T0373676

Digital Media and the Making of Network Temporality

This book presents an exciting new theory of time for a world built on hyper-fast digital media networks. Computers have changed the human social experience enormously. We're becoming familiar with many of the macro changes, but we rarely consider the complex, underlying mechanics of how a technology interacts with our social, political and economic worlds. And we cannot explain how the mechanics of a technology are being translated into social influence unless we understand the role of time in that process.

Offering an original reconsideration of temporality, Philip Pond explains how super-powerful computers and global webs of connection have remade time through speed. The book introduces key developments in network time theory and explains their importance, before presenting a new model of time which seeks to reconcile the traditionally separate subjective and objective approaches to time theory and measurement.

Philip Pond is Lecturer in Digital Media Research Methods at the University of Melbourne. He has written extensively about the relationship between digital technology, speed and informational crisis and his previous book explores the systemic causes of post-truth politics. He heads several research projects, including a multidisciplinary effort to document political extremism online and an analysis of the influence of software in accelerating polarisation.

Digital Media and the Making of Network Temporality

Philip Pond

LONDON AND NEW YORK

First published 2021
by Routledge
2 Park Square, Milton Park, Abingdon, Oxon OX14 4RN

and by Routledge
605 Third Avenue, New York, NY 10017

Routledge is an imprint of the Taylor & Francis Group, an informa business

British Library Cataloguing-in-Publication Data
A catalogue record for this book is available from the British Library

Library of Congress Cataloging-in-Publication Data
Names: Pond, Philip, 1981– author.
Title: Digital media and the making of network temporality / Philip Pond.
Description: Abingdon, Oxon ; New York, NY : Routledge, 2021. | Includes bibliographical references and index.
Identifiers: LCCN 2021003672 (print) | LCCN 2021003673 (ebook) | ISBN 9781032004488 (hardback) | ISBN 9781032004471 (paperback) | ISBN 9781003174226 (ebook)
Subjects: LCSH: Information technology—Social aspects. | Time—Sociological aspects. | Digital media—Social aspects.
Classification: LCC HM851 .P6559 2021 (print) | LCC HM851 (ebook) | DDC 303.48/33—dc23
LC record available at https://lccn.loc.gov/2021003672
LC ebook record available at https://lccn.loc.gov/2021003673

ISBN 13: 978-1-03-200448-8 (hbk)
ISBN 13: 978-1-03-200447-1 (pbk)

Typeset in Times New Roman
by codeMantra

Contents

Figures

Table

1 Network time theory

Introduction

The year 2020 was a difficult one, full of acute traumas and diffuse unease; fire-ravaged, pandemic-ridden and Trump-wrecked. The global population has spent months of the year locked down, under local rules, watching infections spike and deaths inevitably follow. COVID-19 has driven us further into the data-scapes of social media, video conferencing and robotic news production. We have learnt, communed, confessed, worked and mourned online this year. We know that internet companies are collecting more of our secrets than we would share with our loved ones, yet we log on and post. We face the digitisation of our experiences with weary resignation, knowing that eventually automation will destroy our economies of work, but not knowing how to protest that course, let alone change it. Often, it feels inevitable. At times, it has even felt easy.

What were the alternatives? Perhaps we could have withdrawn into our bodies and our homes, our families and the quiet rhythms of closeted days. We could have become more physical with each other, paid more attention to the breath between words, the warmth and the coldness of shared spaces, the slow arc of empty days. We could have aimed for regression, for an older analogue experience, alone with ourselves for a while – but these words sound ridiculous, even as I write them. This is not the world we have built, of course. We log on and check the news because that is where the numbers are reported, the press conferences held, the scandals splashed. The frantic hum of humanity is digital.

Personally, the COVID-19 crisis has been a weirdly disembodied experience, something happening elsewhere, mostly online, more recently in suburbs where I do not live. At some level, I am of course aware that it may spread into my physical experience, but it has not done so yet. For me, it remains a media-thing, a worry in the diffuse or abstract sense. The reaction to it – my city being closed, the loss of work – is far more real and present. Still, the media have my attention. My days revolve around the reporting cycle: the overnight tweets from dystopic America, the morning numbers report, fretful afternoons, bad news from waking Europe and then a few evening hours of Netflix-stupor. All of this happens online for me, mostly through the dull haze of my laptop display, a constant stream of clicks, scrolls and data sales. The news flows, and sometimes I sense that I am flowing back into it. The feeling when the updates stop, when there is no more news for a moment, is really weird. I struggle with the weight of the empty time.

I am not suggesting that COVID-19 is primarily a crisis of time – clearly this is not the case – but I do think that time is implicated in all crises and that we often interpret crises *through time*. This has certainly been the case historically: periods of major disruption or rapid change were often interpreted temporally, largely I expect because people *felt* time shift and reshape itself during these periods (Solnit 2003). A major philosophical development during the twentieth century was the realisation that time is the denominator of human experience (Husserl 1999; McCumber 2011). Being human means being conscious of the world in time, which is both a compelling and a challenging idea. When the world changes, the time of the world also changes, and that means something in the human experience changes with it. The concept of *network time* was developed to help describe and explain some of the most keenly felt changes of the digital age.

This is a book about network time – or, rather, this is a book about that the relationship between two types of time: the time that seems to flow formlessly through the data-scape and the time that confronts us when the flow stops. In this first chapter, I describe what network time is, both in the technical sense and as it relates to social experience, and I try to explain how it comes about as a theory. This requires a couple of things. The first is a brief account of networked computing and the communication practices it supports. Network time is specific to the hyper-fast transfer protocols of the modern internet and the digital data structures upon which they operate. It is hard to understand network time without having some sense of the technology that produces it. Second, it requires a general understanding of social time theory, which develops the idea of time away from the clock and, more broadly, away from the idea of constant universal flow.

In Chapter 2, I explore in far more detail the differences between scientific clock time and the variable times of social experience. This is an important distinction to unpack because the relationship between our different conceptualisations of time has changed. For much of history, scientists and philosophers assumed that they were studying the same phenomenon, even if they chose to approach it very differently; that is no longer the case. Many social theorists agree that they are not interested in the same time as scientists, and many question whether science is really interested in time at all. Indeed, even within the sciences, plenty of researchers hold the view that time is an illusion, a by-product of the human mind's struggle to interpret other physical phenomena. I will examine these ideas and compare them with each other. I want to ask, first, whether there is a thing that we can call time and, second, whether it can be the same thing for both natural and social scientists.

These questions matter because time plays such an important role in our study of change in both natural and social processes, and the measurement of time – particularly in the social sciences – is a very contested idea. Social time theorists have invested considerable resources in demonstrating that the seconds, minutes and hours marked by the clock are themselves constructed through social and technological practices. In effect, they have settled on the idea that social time cannot be measured, and must instead be described through qualitative statements of sense and experience. Scientific time, by contrast, is defined by the practice of measurement, and this distinction is largely responsible for the divergence of the two approaches. In Chapter 3, I look at the possibility of temporal reconciliation, of realigning the social and scientific approaches to time and developing a form of social time measurement. If possible, this would enable social time theorists to use network time as an explanatory variable in their comparative analyses of modern media.

What do we stand to gain from a conceptualisation of network time that supports measurement? This is a question worth asking because we are likely to reveal something important about our temporal thinking in our response. There will be people for whom the concept of time without measurement makes very little sense at all, simply because their conceptualisations of time are so closely bound to the numerical intervals counted by the clock. Clock time is deeply embedded in our social and cultural experiences. It is the hegemonic time within our society and has been since the Industrial Revolution, when labour moved from the field to the factory and required stricter synchronisation (Hassan 2009). Equally, there will be people for whom the distinction between social time and the 'measurable' times of the clock and science is of paramount importance. They will consider my suggestion that social time is measurable nonsense, and see me betraying my ignorance about the phenomenon that the concept describes. For some temporal theorists, the 'impossibility of measurement' is as central to the conceptualisation of social time as the quantification of time is to the scientist.

While this easy categorisation of temporal theorists is helpful, I would suggest that we have more to gain from reconciliation. As I have already noted, the impossibility of measurement limits the explanatory power of social time. I don't say this because I think numbers are necessarily the best way of describing every phenomenon, but rather because the possibility of numbers would enable social time to be deployed comparatively. This is an important point, so it is worth establishing a little more clearly. In Chapter 2, I will spend a little time describing the differences between Bergson's (1999) quantitative and qualitative multiplicities, because this is a distinction upon which a lot of social time theory is predicated. In Bergson's view, some phenomena are measurable because they are effectively repeated instantiations of the same type, and some are not. Time cannot be measured because it falls into the latter category – whereas numbers describe instances of the same thing, the temporal experience at moment n is fundamentally different from the experience at n + 1.

This means that the temporal experience we describe in one context tells us nothing at all about the temporal experience within a different context, even if those contexts are broadly comparable. This is another way of saying that social time has little comparative explanatory power because it is always embedded within the instance of its experience. This is a problem for a couple of reasons. The first is a general issue: the narrow contextualisation of social time makes it an elusive concept. Descriptions of network time, for instance, often seem more focussed on telling us what the phenomenon is *not* rather than describing what it *is*. Manuel Castells (1996: xli) defines his version of network time as 'timeless time' to emphasise the 'systematic perturbation in the sequential order of the social practices'. Weltevrede et al. (2014: 129) call network time 'a "non-time" without past and without duration'. These descriptions agree that network time is very fast, but beyond this characterisation they focus on temporal features that appear not to be absent from network time. Ultimately, discussions of network time tend to become generalised discussions about temporal theory rather than being discrete, objective descriptions of a phenomenon unfolding in the world. Network time becomes the confounding of the theorist's temporal expectations. The temporal challenge, as it is presented, is to the theorist's understanding of social time: that is the principal phenomenon under review.

The second issue is a critique of how social time is used in social theory. Also in Chapter 2, I will explore these ideas in more detail. For now, let's say simply that social time theorists tend to focus on qualitative descriptions of temporal experience for the social categories that interest them. While this framing sounds banal, it really is not. It means that social time is realised through the established practices of social research, which tend to be focussed on specific roles or practices within the established schema of social theory. Descriptions of different social times exist for different types of labour (academic time, for instance), and for different cultural modes (leisure time), institutions, technologies and media – in other words, for all the different categories that tend to attract social researchers.

There is a logical contradiction implicit within this sorting of social times into neat contextual categories. If social time is truly contextual, born entirely within a specific phenomenon, and truly impossible to measure, it cannot also be shared by individual instances within a category. For instance, the category of academic time envelops hundreds of thousands of academics globally in a shared temporal experience, when those academics work in multitudinous different ways, to different rhythms and with highly variable rewards for each unit of their labour-time. Any sense of a shared academic time, then, is dependent on a massive reduction in this complexity and the description of a few dominant threads or trends in shared practice. Once the possibility of sharing is introduced, the logic of contextual instantiation breaks down; the impossibility of measurement becomes impossible itself. If there is temporal sharing between units within a temporal category, then this surely implies that the thing being shared must be continuous between those units. In other words, there must be an objective phenomenon that is being shared between contexts, and we must be able to recognise it as the same phenomenon. This rather suggests that the time being shared is a repeated instantiation of the same type, which means it must be countable.

To my mind, this logical uncertainty should be untenable, especially if we accept that time is the denominator of experience, the variable that underwrites our interactions in the world. This is why I think reconciliation is desirable, even necessary, and we should be working to ensure that social and scientific time theorists can understand each other. In Chapter 3, I argue that reconciliation may be possible, provided that we rethink some of our longstanding assumptions about objective reality. This 'rethinking' is the major theoretical contribution of the book, and it requires a rejection of object-permanence in favour of an ontological model based around systemic change. Rejection is, perhaps, not the ideal word here, because it implies a dramatic break with object-permanence, suggesting that is currently a universally accepted view and that, of course, is not the case. System-theoretical models of change are already well established in both the physical and the social sciences and my main contribution here is simply to observe similarities between them – and to wonder if these similarities might be aligned more closely.

In physics, quantum theories of time are predicated on probabilistic systemic becoming. In Niklas Luhmann's social system theory, time is located within the differentiation processes of discrete systems, part of the 'interpretation of reality with regard to the difference between past and future' (Luhmann 1976: 135). Are the systems of physicists and the systems of social scientists fundamentally so different? My suggestion is that they are not, and my aim is to show that a discrete set of quantifiable events can produce multiple subjective experiences, assuming those events are located within a wider field of systemic interaction. Most of Chapter 3 is spent establishing these ideas, identifying and explaining the shared principles of scientific and social time, and uniting these principles within a general model of systemic time.

In Chapter 4 and again in Chapter 5, I return to the concept of network time and ask what it might look reinterpreted according to the principles of systemic time theory. There are several steps in this process. First, I consider what sort of events are implicated in the assemblage of the network system. These events are key markers of change within the network – under the system model, time is produced through change events as part of the systemic differentiation process. Using empirical examples, I show how change is produced from interactions between different components of the network system: users, code, data, discourse and so on. I establish a method for identifying and recording these interaction events and assigning them a value for temporal comparison.

Unfortunately, the reconciliation of the subjective and scientific approaches to network time is more complicated than simply identifying a set of relevant events that can be accepted by both sets of theorists. In the second and final part of the chapter, I discuss the various complexities that we must address in order to synthesise multiple perspectives within the network to produce a representative measure of system time. This discussion revisits the key principles identified in Chapter 3 and applies them to concrete empirical examples. So, for instance, I discuss what it means for the production of time if a Twitter conversation has ten rather than 10,000 active participants, I establish the variable significance of application programming interfaces (APIs) for network time calculation and I discuss the role of media logics in shaping the temporal rhythms of the digital-data-scape. At the end of this process, I hope I will have established that it is at least feasible to consider the reconciliation of scientific and subjective times around a shared understanding of interactive systems.

Network time theory

Network time is a concept with many overlapping definitions. The earliest iterations of network time theory arose through analyses of the globalisation processes that were transforming human societies acutely towards the end of the twentieth century. Many of these analyses will be familiar because they made their authors famous. David Harvey (1990), Anthony Giddens (1990) and Manuel Castells (1996), for instance, all found ways to interpret dramatic social changes through the compression of temporal and spatial relationships: 'The dynamism of modernity derives from the *separation of time and space* and their recombination in forms which permit the precise time-space "zoning" of social life' (Giddens 1990: 16–17).

While globalisation clearly happens across multiple domains of human experience – consider the five dimensions of Arjun Appadurai's (1991) global-cultural flow – all these authors implicate the media, and electronic media particularly, at the heart of the process. Consider, for instance, David Harvey's (1990: 292) analysis of the impact of mass broadcast media, which disturbed the relationship between presence and absence in profound ways, 'collapsing the world's space into a series of images on a television screen'. For Castells (1996: xxxii), networked computing is a communication revolution reconfiguring all aspects of human experience, transforming 'the spatiality of social interaction by introducing simultaneity, or any chosen timeframe, in social practices, regardless of the actors engaged in the communication process'. This transformation in spatial relations has temporal effects as well, and Castells (1996: xli) provides one of the earliest iterations of a network time theory, predicated on the 'systematic perturbation in the sequential order of the social practices' performed in a given context.

What does this mean? Analysts of globalisation, which is probably the dominant social dynamic of the past 50 years, have repeatedly suggested that the process is characterised by changes that have profound spatial and temporal effects. Those all tend in the same direction, towards what Harvey called time-space compression: exchange becomes quicker, distance becomes less inhibitory, the pace of social practice is increased, the rhythms of social experience become more frenetic. We can look to a range of activities to prove these trends. The mass movement of people around the globe on jet aircraft has reduced travel times from several months to a matter of hours, and enabled transformative economic and social migration. The electrification of financial markets has reduced transaction times to mere fractions of a second, transforming investment practices and super-charging capital flows between capitalist power-hubs. In 2008, the collapse of Lehmann Brothers illustrated quite clearly how the mass interconnection of debt and debt-fuelled transaction could be brought to a shuddering halt in a frighteningly short time. The past decade has shown that the global domination of mass media corporations like News Corporation and Facebook spawns democratic crises in nation-states regardless of geography and history. The world seems compressed and it seems quickened, and though these trends may be extensions of '*traditional* global connection' (James 2006: 22), they are profoundly challenging for the traditional orders of practice.

This is the global-social context within which network time theory is realised. The internet (more precisely, the networked infrastructure of microelectronic computing machines) is at the vanguard of these globalisation processes, both in the popular imagination and in academic analysis. The massive speeds of the global financial market are only possible because of modern computing power and networked communication protocols. So, before we move on to consider the precise characteristics of network time, it is important to ensure that we understand the properties of the technology that is meant to realise it, particularly given this background of global-cultural flow.

Network time is the temporal experience of networked computers and their communication (Hassan 2003). For many theorists, the speed of network time is almost directly reducible to the speed (and power) of the modern automated processor, making it 'a *qualitatively* different form of time from its technological predecessor' (Hassan 2009: 67). Network time is hyper-fast because modern computers perform calculations incredibly quickly and communicate the results of those calculations almost instantaneously. Modern 'media and communications technologies have transformed time into a revolutionary new mode characterised by speed and immediacy' (Keightley 2012: 3). As David Berry (2011b: 97–98) writes:

> Although the clocks within microprocessors 'tick' very quickly, this is propagated around the system to provide an internal formatting which allows different parts of the system to work together. Each tick is the execution of a single instruction, that is why the processor speed (in GHz) tells you something useful about the computer; in other words, how fast it processes instructions in real-time ... the temporality of code is much faster than the temporality of the everyday.

The technical term for delay in this transfer is *latency*, and latency is incredibly low in modern computers and in the infrastructure that they support – technologies like the internet. I think low latency inspires metaphors of temporal 'collapse' or 'annihilation' largely because we *feel* time more acutely while we are 'waiting' for it to pass. Rebecca Solnit (2003) has documented how the expansion of the railroad across the North American continent quickened travel, so that journeys that had once taken weeks or months could be accomplished in a few days. She describes how disorientating that *transformation of waiting* was for the people who first experienced it:

> Thirty-five miles an hour was nearly as fast as the fastest horse, and unlike a gallop, it could be sustained almost indefinitely. It was a dizzying speed. Passengers found the landscape out the train windows was blurred, impossible to contemplate, erased by speeds that would now seem a slow crawl to us. Those who watched the trains approach sometimes thought they were physically getting larger, because the perceptual change in a large object approaching at that speed was an unprecedented phenomenon. Ulysses S. Grant remembered riding on one of the early railroads in Pennsylvania in 1839 with the same amazement that most early travelers recorded: 'We traveled at

> least eighteen miles an hour when at full speed, and made the whole distance averaging as much as twelve miles an hour. This seemed like annihilating space.'
>
> (Solnit 2003: 9–10)

Solnit (2003: 11) argues that the 'annihilation' of time and space is 'what most new technologies aspire to do', principally through the reconfiguration of 'communications and transportation'. The temporal environment produced by computers can thus be seen as a culmination of centuries of techno-social transformation, beginning with the Industrial Revolution when workers were moved from the field into machine-regulated factories and workhouses (Hassan 2009). The rhythms of these new workplaces were measured by the clock, and so were the lives of the workers. Labour became a time-commodity, and was increasingly synchronised in pursuit of productivity. The 'natural' diurnal and seasonal rhythms of agriculture were subsumed into the rigid calendar of industry, much as rural people were subsumed into the heaving industrial towns and cities. These work-rhythms were the antecedents of network time. In the late eighteenth and early nineteenth centuries, populations in Europe and North America had their lives transformed by sweeping economic and social changes that were made possible by machines and reinforced by them. Steam power, the railway and later electrification and automation mangled social, familial and biological times through the grinding churn of industrial production. Fordist capitalism, mass media and world wars accelerated these trends through the twentieth century, strengthening the hegemony of clock time and its tight schedules, and highly calibrated, granular periods (Armitage 1999; Virilio 1977). In this historical arc, network time is the rhythm of the post-industrial age, of the late twentieth and early twenty-first centuries, where capital and labour flows have been made global and digitised.

At this point, it is important to differentiate between network time, being the *experience* of networked computers and digital communication, and the same term used by engineers to describe the protocols that synchronise *action* within these networks. Google 'network time' and the majority of the responses will relate to this second usage – the science of network time involves the calibration of highly accurate clocks and the regulation of data transfer between nodes in the network (Mills 1991). Of course, the two forms of network time are distinct but also very much interrelated. The action enabled by network time protocols produces the experience of network time discussed in this book. It is the difference between the two ideas, the gap between the mechanical action of the clocks and the variable experience of the network, that so interests (social) network time theorists. More confusingly, instead of 'network time', some social theorists use the term 'real time' (e.g. Weltevrede et al. 2014) to describe particular features of network time, especially the apparent erasure of any sorting of waiting or delay. This sense of immediacy is also emphasised by Castells (1996) in his description of 'timeless time'. I am using the term 'network time' to refer to all these social ideas. If I wish to refer to network synchronisation in the mechanical sense, I will refer to network time protocols.

Network time is fast because computers are fast, but surely there must be more to the sociotechnical analysis than this; otherwise, there would be no need to differentiate network time from other hyper-fast experiences in twenty-first-century societies. Paul Virilio argues that acceleration lies at the heart of modern social organisation and transformation. *Dromology*, which is the 'relentless logic' of speed, underwrites measures of urban space and social progress, so that in addition to a political economy of wealth, we must also acknowledge that there is a political economy of speed (Armitage 1999). In Virilio's telling, this is also a military logic, the creep of hyper-fast warfare into all corners of social governance and architectural planning: 'Everything in this new warfare becomes a question of time won by man over the fatal projectiles toward which his path throws him' (Virilio 1977: 46). The logic is inescapable, hardwired almost into social forms and political institutions: 'Governance by speed (by states or otherwise) is *logistics*, and logistics, like the oceanic vectors from which it is born, is omnidirectional' (Bratton 2006: 12).

In addition to being fast, network time is complex in ways that defy easy explanation. Manuel Castells (1996) characterises computational time as *timeless* because in addition to being fast it presents as non-linear, somehow disturbing or distorting the expected order of events. Weltevrede and colleagues (2014: 129) call network time 'a "non-time" without past and without duration' because the internet supports massive data flows that seem to assemble in different places all at once. This is a disorientating whirl of events, in which everything seems to happen simultaneously, and the orderly structures of temporal experience feel absent. In part, of course, this disorientation is a function of the speed of computational action and the volume of data processing that the architecture supports, but there are multidimensional features of network time that speed alone cannot explain. Some theorists suggest that network time is multiple speeds all at once (Pond 2020b), while others emphasise the disembodied disorientations of the digital experience: 'Much that was once analogue "natural" in our communicative practice has become digital "atmospheric"' (Hassan 2018: 8). I said previously that it was necessary to understand something about networked computing technology in order to understand the 'shape' of network time, so what are the particular characteristics or features of the technology that might be implicated here?

Technology and time

There are three technological dimensions to network time that I want to highlight, but first it is important to say that I do not think these technologies are sufficient on their own to explain the shape of network time. That is to say, I am not proposing a deterministic relationship between the technology and the time that shares its name. Rather, I think the description and analysis of technology within society must proceed with a dual intent, much like the philosopher Andrew Feenberg (2005) has described in instrumentalisation theory. It must capture and assess the functional features or 'affordances' of a technology, but it must also consider the contextualising information (ethical, cultural, aesthetic) that 'qualifies the original functionalization by orienting it toward a new world involving those same objects and subjects' (Feenberg 2005: 51).

The first of the three technological dimensions is automation. All computers are automatons – machines built to perform repetitive tasks on information following programmable instructions. Automation can be considered a 'super logic' of the modern internet (Pond 2020a) and is centrally implicated in the speed of network time: the faster that a computer performs the repetitive actions of an automated task, the faster the temporal experience it can produce. Modern processors are capable of performing thousands of actions every second, and the modern internet connects millions of computers in vast networks to supercharge the automated processing of data.

What is a network? In the simplest sense, it is a connection between computers – usually multiple computers able to send and receive data 'packets' and to perform operations on that data. The internet is descended from the Advanced Research Projects Agency Network (ARPANET), a military network created as a Cold War defence system (Abbate 2000; Leiner et al. 2009). Various technologies exist that enable computers to communicate with each other over vast distances, and of course these include the physical cables and wires that carry the electrical signals of digital transmission. They also include the packet switching and communication protocols that allow vast quantities of digital data to be encoded and sent through these signals. An entire field of data science is dedicated to the study of information transfer, its integrity and stability (Shannon and Weaver 1949).

In part, network time is so dynamic and variable because so many computers are connected to the network at once, performing different actions on different data but all adding to (and interacting with) the massive global flows of electrical information. Some of these actions are incredibly fast while some are far slower, and it is this disjuncture between connected responses that so complicates the experience of network time. For instance, Gehl (2011) points to the contrasting dynamics of the processor and 'the archive': while modern processors are incredibly fast, as we have discussed, the product of that processing – vast digital data structures – can persist unchanged in storage, largely forgotten, waiting as if out of time for a moment of immediate retrieval.

Networking works in harness with automation to drive both the speed and the expansive logics of network time. In their analysis of social media technologies, van Dijck and Poell (2013) highlight the *connective urgency* of these media, which are always seeking new nodes to add to the network. In large part, the profit models of the corporations behind these media tools are founded on such expansionary growth, either through the addition of new users or through increased 'interaction' with existing actors. The neoliberal logic of 'parallel acceleration in exchange and consumption' (Harvey 1990: 285) is thus implicated as a central dynamic in network time, which is why so many authors consider it a hyper-charged culmination of postmodern capitalism.

What is particularly postmodern about this form of capitalism? The question is worth considering because the data produced by digital action have peculiar properties that add a third technical dimension to network time. Robert Hassan (2018) describes a fundamental difference between digital and analogue production systems. Whereas analogue systems are predicated on their recognisable representation of the physical or 'natural' world, digital systems are different: 'Having no recognisable analogue in nature means that we do not easily grasp, or recognise, what digital does at the technology-human-environment level' (Hassan 2018: 7). In other words, automation inscribes digital systems with a self-reflective logic; this is profoundly different from systems that prioritise analogue ways of knowing themselves – the digital exists principally in reference to itself and thus produces meaning in a sense that can feel separate and disorientating. Lev Manovich (2003) describes how new media become digital data *controlled* by software, so that deferral and dissociation are captured by the infinite *variability* possible in hypertext. This heightens the sense of network time being a time apart, or a time separate from and disjunctive to the time of the clock and the rhythms of biological experience.

This is why descriptions of network time often emphasise detachment – the sense of temporal vortex, of rhythms neither biological nor mechanical, the profound lack of feeling inherent to the experience. In some sense, we consider network time particularly worthy of study because we consider it unlike other times – it feels different. Additionally, of course, it is new and increasingly, it seems, taking over. Robert Hassan (2016) used the term 'hegemonic time' when he described the dominating influence of the clock in industrial society. A hegemonic time is one that achieves widespread social acculturation, becoming *the time* against which all the variable rhythms of personal, economic and political life are paced. Before the clock, the daily and seasonal rhythms of agriculture dominated.

Network time is social

Note that we are talking about time here as though it exists in several 'forms' all at once. I have mentioned social and biological times, for instance, and described these different times being mangled together through industrial churn, then measured and commodified by the clock. The concept of a hegemonic time relies upon one time dominating *other times*. How does this make any sort of sense, given that we are used to thinking about time as something abstract and independent from us, that 'flows' forwards regardless, advancing uniformly towards the future while the past trails in its wake?

The larger subject of time theory and the differentiation between different types of time is the subject of Chapter 2, so I will not say too much about here. If readers are familiar with special relativity, even in outline, they may already know that Einstein showed how clocks would run slow at very fast speeds, and realise that the independent-uniform view of time is not quite right. However, we need to complicate our understanding of time still further because network time is an example of social time theory, which asserts that time is altogether more variable and more complex than Einstein would have allowed. Social time theorists argue that time actually exists as a different phenomenon. They call the time that Einstein described and argued for 'scientific time' and distinguish it from 'social time', which is broadly understood as a more experiential, embodied, even emotional phenomenon. The idea that there might be different social times, each peculiar to a different set of practices or experiences, is perhaps best captured by Barbara Adam's (1998: 10) concept of *timescapes*:

> Where other scapes such as landscapes, cityscapes and seascapes mark the spatial features of past and present activities and interactions of organisms and matter, timescapes emphasise their rhythmicities, their timings and tempos, their changes and contingencies... Timescapes are thus the embodiment of practiced approaches to time.

The French sociologist Henri Lefebvre also emphasised the rhythms of social life in his work on time and temporal experience. According to Lefebvre (1992), the study of social time is an exercise in 'rhythmanalysis', or the pacing of the cyclical and linear rhythms that characterise the repetitive happenings of the social world. Think of a city and the daily pulsing of traffic and people, gridlock and flow, commuters spurting from trains, residents circling the emptying streets with their dogs, the swings between quiet hum and clamour (Lefebvre 1992). These are the events that give time its shape and flavour that locate it as something *in the world*, rather than something abstract and elsewhere. These are the events that social time theorists try to describe.

Behind these descriptions, of course, are deeper questions about what time is and how time works, which we will eventually have to address if we are going to explore network time fully. For now, though, it will suffice to note that the concept of network time is predicated on this type of qualitative description: we are interested in the events that give shape and flavour to the experience of time in networks.

So what are the informational and experiential events through which network time is constructed? It is a little surprising that there is not yet a huge amount of empirical description available to help us identify and describe these events. After all, the internet is a highly *datafied* environment. Most users will be aware of how a company like Facebook can follow them as they move around the web, exchanging tracking information with their browser, silently monitoring their scrolls and their clicks and the information they retrieve. That sort of data collection is ubiquitous online, so it might seem as if we would be well placed to monitor (and even measure) the event-based construction of network time if we were inclined to do so. That hasn't really happened, though – most of the analysis is focussed on the sensation of network time, its overwhelming speed, its immediacy and its sometimes confounding variability. The experience of network time is more commonly described through abstraction and literary flourishes. Network time users are always pressed by the demands of immediacy, stuck in an 'eternal now' (Uprichard 2012), spinning through dense information streams and data flows (Berry 2011a; Weltevrede et al. 2014).

This may be because such a clear distinction is made between the hyper-fast mechanical time of the computers themselves and the hyper-fast malleable time of the user experience. Many platforms and websites deploy careful presentational massaging of their mechanical impulses, which seems to muddle and confuse discrete temporal events into a miasmic swirl of temporal uncertainty. Furthermore, when users interact with this uncertainty, they do so from their own private-subjective perspectives, which makes it harder still to describe any sort of shared network time experience.

Network time study

There have only been a few attempts to pull this sensory environment apart and to look more closely at its workings, and these have tended to view network time as a product of informational flow. For instance, Weltevrede et al. (2014: 130) argue that the web 'actually produces specific temporalities through its engines, platforms and their web cultures' and that we therefore 'need to consider the interrelation between experience and processing and will do so by engaging with a device perspective which explores the interplay between technicity, actors, practices and experience of web devices'. This leads them to study network time through the pacing of publication in different device-specific ecosystems, predominantly those created by Western social media and search conglomerates.

In this view, the 'pace' of the different platforms is defined by the speed at which they update with new content, so the production of time is conflated with the production of device-specific content units. For instance, the Google search engine is paced by the number of novel results it returns in response to a predefined query; Twitter is paced by the number of tweets published containing the query-phrase; Facebook is timed by the number of posts published, and so on. In order to standardise the approach and to compare the pace of the different platforms, a comparative measure is calculated by counting the number of new content units within five-minute periods. The outcome of the Weltevrede et al. (2014) approach is displayed as a series of vertical lines crowded along an x-axis measuring five-minute increments: the results look a little like extended barcodes. The denser the clustering of the vertical lines, the faster time is happening on the platform. The authors use this approach to identify different 'types' of time that they suggest are shared across the platforms:

> the findings of the case study suggest that there are indeed different patterns of pace. Pace is not only connected to the algorithmic logic of the device but also to the different types of web activities such as posting, linking, editing, sharing, uploading and retweeting that are connected to each device. Platforms and engines allow for different activities that contribute to the specific pace of a device.
>
> (Weltevrede et al. 2014: 138)

These different patterns of pace are grouped into three types that differentiate the devices: stream pace, bulk pace and stale pace. Social media channels that frequently engage their users display stream pace, meaning that content is updated continuously. To re-use the language of David Berry (2011b), these devices tick incessantly. Bulk pace describes devices that update in spurts of new content, normally when users upload material 'in batches' on to 'content platforms such as Flickr … Google News, where editors follow news cycles, or in Wikipedia, where edits tend to be done in batches as users often save multiple minor edits to a single article within a short timeframe' (Weltevrede et al. 2014: 140). Stale pace is displayed by devices that update content irregularly, *relative to the standardised five-minute comparison period*. Obviously this tends to be linked to the type of content that the platform publishes: blog posts demand more labour than tweets, take longer and so update less frequently.

What value is there in separating the publication habits of different web platforms into different pace patterns like this? The authors suggest that it 'allows us to give an account of the making of real-time which does not unfold as a flat, eternal now' (Weltevrede et al. 2014: 140), but instead highlights the different events and actions that produce time on specific platforms. In other words, the benefit of these pace calculations is that they unflatten the temporal experience, illustrating that network time is not uniform throughout the network. They emphasise that network time is local and contextual, a product of specific events happening in specific contexts, producing particular rhythms that can be analysed. As a result, the authors 'suggest thinking about time online not as events happening *in* real-time, in the now, but as being entangled in the fabrication of specific forms of real-time*ness*' (Weltevrede et al. 2014: 143). Time is not a container into which events are placed, but rather something produced through the events happening, a live and emergent phenomenon intimately tied to local experiences.

Other studies have adopted similar approaches in an attempt to locate and describe instances of network time. The periodic pacing of content production just described is an example of a time-series analysis, which is a common enough approach in web social science, where it is often used to compare the popularity of different themes or topics over time (e.g. Thelwall 2014, 2016; Vilares et al. 2015). Such approaches 'use timestamps (which are assigned on publication to all tweets) to organise data into intervals of regular duration, which can then be displayed graphically as a histogram' (Pond 2020b: 5). Such techniques are often used to describe the temporality of social media feeds. Pond and Lewis (2019) combine a series of time-series analyses of different discourses on Twitter to describe the temporality of public discussion during periods of acute social unrest. They then analyse relations between different types of events and identify certain factors that seem particularly influential on the production of Twitter time. Actions by high-profile or popular accounts, for instance, seem to prompt cascades of further events, massively speeding up the pace of the discourse. The authors speculate that this speeding up can have consequences for the direction in which the discourse is headed: the platform responds algorithmically to increased pace and certain types of discourse are preferred over others. The effect presumably has problematic consequences for the public sphere.

However, in their attempt to compare the influence of different events on the production of Twitter time, the authors realise that, if network time is user-driven and event-based, then it is surely too simplistic to describe it using publication rates. The problem is that not all publication is temporally equal. We have mentioned already that a blog post is temporally very different from a tweet: it takes longer to produce, but it also takes longer to consume, so it *persists* in the network very differently. This is an issue for making comparisons between different platforms but it is also an issue within a real-time culture. Pond and Lewis (2019) argue that not all tweets are temporally equal either in part because they are handled differently by the Twitter algorithms but also because tweets have inherent attributes that make them temporally very different. Publication on Twitter is not a singular experience: the follow–following dynamic that is so central to Twitter's character means that publication is different for every user of the platform. A tweet published by a user with many follows is published in each of those followers' timelines, perhaps instantiated millions of times over, whereas an account with zero followers publishes only in a technical sense to a curious non-space – the tweet may never be viewed by another Twitter user.

This creates a couple of problems. First, it means that the description of network time is an incredibly complex task requiring the interpretative analysis of huge numbers of events involving both human and non-human users. Identifying those events is an enormous undertaking, and so is synthesising them into a coherent account of temporal experience. Second, it means that even within device-specific cultures, network time remains highly variable, possibly existing as multiple streams at once, fragmenting with the platform audience into discrete and different temporal experiences. This second point, of course, is one of the central assertions of social time theory – time exists in the experience of the subject, which means time itself is different for different subjects. This is a considerable challenge for network time theory. How is it possible to define and describe a phenomenon if that phenomenon presents differently to anyone with access to it?

This latter point could call into question the sense of the entire network time concept, on the grounds that it is an attempt to unify a temporal experience that is too discordant and too contextual to be unified. The same issue was flagged earlier in the chapter – any sense of a shared network time is dependent on a massive reduction in its complexity and the description of a few dominant threads or trends in shared practice. Pond and Lewis (2019) suggest that this might be achievable through a conceptual reworking of network time as an 'atmospheric' or ambient experience. They borrow the concept of 'ambient discourse' from boyd et al. (2010) to describe the sense of being 'surrounded' online by meaning-making activity on a platform like Twitter: 'ambience has to engage with the temporality of tweet publication: what matters is the relative concentration of topical tweets within a specific data sample collected during a specific period' (Pond and Lewis 2019: 222). Network time is thus reduced to the ambient sense of pace on a platform for a given period, where pace is a function of the average speed of interactivity on that platform. This is a useful idea, not so much because it reveals the full complexity of network time, but because it suggests it may be possible to assess different events temporally in terms of their influence on this ambient 'averaged' time.

For instance, as we have already noted, actions by popular social media users tend to have a far greater influence over ambient platform activity than actions by unpopular users. Under these circumstances, it does not make a huge amount of sense to treat all tweets, posts or comments as temporally the same because user popularity clearly contributes to very different ambient effects. Should we attempt to adjust for these effects when we try to summarise network time and, if so, how should we do this? Are especially popular tweets 'worth' more temporally? If so, how does this additive effect work? The authors propose some adjustments to the publication model of network time that are meant to account for the way user attributes such as popularity shape the *persistence* of content on a platform, but these are preliminary steps only. The larger issue is that we cannot begin to answer these sorts of questions unless we already have a clear idea of what network time is, how it works and the way it exerts influence in the world.

For instance, what if we wanted to describe the temporal consequences of the impact of COVID-19 on our social, economic and political lives? Consider how difficult this question is even in abstract terms. How much more complex would it be to try to assess the temporal impact of the disease, to make it an *explanatory variable* in our analyses of the emergent social order? The question demands that we compare two times, before and after COVID-19, identify differences between those times, then connect those differences to social, economic and political outcomes. The problem with the social theorisation of time, however, is that our descriptions of pre- and post-COVID times will be entirely contextual, dependent on the places and the practices of the people experiencing those times. We may well find that there is just as much variation within our pre- and post-COVID categories as there is between them. We can frame this challenge in different terms. When we try to use time as an explanatory variable in social theory, we find quite quickly that the *impossibility of measurement* also makes empirical comparison impossible. Despite our belief – and our historical reasoning – that time is the denominator of our experiences, we cannot access time in a way that allows us to use it to explain phenomena.

This is particularly frustrating when we simultaneously hold the view that time is a fundamental consideration whenever we think about change of any type – the problem seems impossible. On the one hand, unless time has variability, contextuality and discrete characteristics, it serves no explanatory purpose anyway – something that is always the same everywhere doesn't explain difference. On the other hand, if time is defined by difference, then we face all the explanatory challenges we have just discussed – a variable that always varies with context is also always confounded by context: time is simply unavailable empirically for comparative analysis.

So what should we do with time in general, and with network time in particular? At present, our position appears to contain several contradictions. Time is vital and elusive, everywhere and always different. These contradictions are why social scientists and natural scientists, when they talk about time, often seem to be referencing entirely different things. *Scientific time* is universal and mathematical; *social time* is local and experiential. In the next chapter, we will look more closely at the scientific and the social positions, explore their shared origin and explain the circumstances that led to their bifurcation. This will provide an important context for Chapter 3, which aims to establish some parameters for the reconciliation of the two approaches. Reconciliation, I will argue, is highly desirable.

The preceding discussion reveals contradictions within the conceptualisation of network time that are limiting. It also establishes that these limitations are worth addressing. Remember that network time does not arise from abstract or theoretical discussion about time, but from our collective, lived experience of this hypermediated twenty-first century. The network surrounds us; we have to live with its different rhythms, symbolically and emotionally but also materially. It shapes our work, our finances, our politics, our communities and our friendships. It is challenging our relationship with time in ways that demand a response. For decades, we have been adapting to the hegemony of network time without fully considering the implications. In recent years, we have discovered threats to our emotional and physical wellbeing, our social institutions and our democratic processes (Hassan 2012). The COVID-19 crisis further exposes the fragility of our adopted timescapes; it has never been more necessary to establish a cogent and communicable understanding of this phenomenon.

References

Abbate, J. (2000) *Inventing the Internet*. Cambridge, MA: MIT Press.

Adam, B. (1998) *Timescapes of Modernity: The Environment and Invisible Hazards*. London: Routledge.

Appadurai, A. (1991) Disjuncture and difference in the global cultural economy. *Theory Culture Society*, 7, pp. 295–310.

Armitage, J. (1999) Paul Virilio: An introduction. *Theory, Culture & Society*, 16, pp. 1–23.

Bergson, H. (1999 [1922]) *Duration and Simultaneity*. Manchester: Clinamen Press.

Berry, D. (2011a) Messianic media: Notes on the real-time stream. Available at: http://stunlaw.blogspot.com.au/2011/09/messianic-media-notes-on-real-time.html. Accessed 20 December 2020.

Berry, D. (2011b) *The Philosophy of Software: Code and Mediation in the Digital Age*. London: Palgrave Macmillan.

boyd, d., Golder, S. and Lotan, G. (2010) Tweet, tweet, retweet: Conversational aspects of retweeting on Twitter. Paper presented at System Sciences (HICSS), 2010 43rd Hawaii International Conference. Honolulu.

Bratton, B. (2006) Logistics of habitual circulation: A brief introduction to the 2006 edition of *Speed and Politics*. In P. Virilio (ed.), *Speed and Politics*, 2nd ed., trans M. Polizzotti. New York: Semiotext(e), pp. 7–25.

Castells, M. (1996) *The Rise of the Networked Society*. Oxford: Blackwell.

Feenberg, A. (2005) Critical theory of technology: An overview. *Tailoring Biotechnologies*, 1(1), pp. 47–64.

Gehl, R.W. (2011) The archive and the processor: The internal logic of Web 2.0. *New Media & Society*, 13, pp. 1228–44.

Giddens, A. (1990) *The Consequences of Modernity*. Cambridge: Polity Press.

Harvey, D. (1990) *The Condition of Postmodernity: An Enquiry into the Origins of Cultural Change*. Oxford: Blackwell.

Hassan, R. (2003) Network time and the new knowledge epoch. *Time and Society*, 12: 225–41.

Hassan, R. (2009) *Empires of Speed: Time and the Acceleration of Politics and Society*. Leiden: Brill.

Hassan, R. (2012) Not ready for democracy: Social networking and the power of the people. The revolts of 2011 in a temporalized context. *Arab Media & Society*, 26 March. Available at: www.arabmediasociety.com/not-ready-for-democracy-social-networking-and-the-power-of-the-people-the-revolts-of-2011-in-a-temporalized-context. Accessed 10 October 2014.

Hassan, R. (2016) Time and sovereignty in the neoliberal hegemony. In P. Huebener, S. O'Brien, T. Porter, L. Stockdale and Y.R. Zhou (eds), *Time, Globalization and Human Experience*. London: Routledge, pp. 34–46.

Hassan, R. (2018) There isn't an app for that: Analogue and digital politics in the age of platform capitalism. *Media Theory*, 2, pp. 1–28.
Husserl, E. (1999) *The Essential Husserl: Basic Writings in Transcendental Phenomenology*. Bloomington: Indiana University Press.
James, P. (2006) *Globalism, Nationalism, Tribalism*. London: Sage.
Keightley, E. (2012) Introduction: Time, media, modernity. In E. Keightley (ed.), *Time, Media, Modernity*. London: Palgrave Macmillan, pp. 1–24.
Lefebvre, H. (1992) *Rhythmanalysis: Space, Time and Everyday Life*. London: Bloomsbury.
Leiner, B., Cerf, V.G., Clark, D.D., Kahn, R.E., Kelinrock, L., Lynch, D.C., Postel, J., Roberts L.G. and Wolff, S. (2009) A brief history of the internet. *Computer Communication Review*, 39, pp. 22–31.
Luhmann, N. (1976) The future cannot begin: Temporal structures in modern society. *Social Research*, 43(1), pp. 130–52.
Manovich, L. (2003) New media from Borges to HTML. In N. Wardrip-Fruin and N. Montfort (eds), *The New Media Reader*. Cambridge, MA: MIT Press, pp. 13–16.
McCumber, J. (2011) *Time and Philosophy: A History of Continental Thought*. Durham, NC: Acumen.
Mills, D.L. (1991) Internet time synchronization: The network time protocol. *IEEE Transactions on Communications*, 39, pp. 1482–93.
Pond, P. (2020a) *Complexity, Digital Media and Post Truth Politics: A Theory of Interactive Systems*. Cham: Palgrave Macmillan.
Pond, P. (2020b) An event-based model for studying network time empirically in digital media systems. *New Media & Society*, https://doi.org/10.1177/1461444820911711.
Pond, P. and Lewis, J. (2019) Riots and Twitter: Connective politics, social media and framing discourses in the digital public sphere. *Information, Communication & Society*, 22(2), pp. 213–31.
Shannon, C. and Weaver, W. (1949) *The Mathematical Theory of Communication*. Urbana: University of Illinois Press.
Solnit, R. (2003) The annihilation of time and space. *New England Review*, 24(1), pp. 5–19.
Thelwall, M. (2014) Sentiment analysis and time series with Twitter. In K. Weller, A. Bruns, J. Burgess, M. Mahrt and C. Puschmann (eds), *Twitter and Society*. New York: Peter Lang, pp. 83–95.
Thelwall, M. (2016) Web indicators for research evaluation: A practical guide. *Synthesis Lectures on Information Concepts, Retrieval, and Services*, 8. Available at: https://www.morganclaypool.com/doi/abs/10.2200/S00733ED1V01Y201609ICR052. Accessed 29 December 2020.
Uprichard, E. (2012) Being stuck in (live) time: The sticky sociological imagination. *The Sociological Review*, 60(1), pp. 124–38.
van Dijck, J. and Poell, T. (2013) Understanding social media logic. *Media and Communication*, 1(1), pp. 2–14.

Vilares, D., Thelwall, M. and Alonso, M.A. (2015) The megaphone of the people? Spanish SentiStrength for real-time analysis of political tweets. *Journal of Information Science*, 41, pp. 799–813.

Virilio, P. (1977) *Speed and Politics.* New York: Semiotext(e).

Weltevrede, E., Helmond, A. and Gerlitz, C. (2014) The politics of real-time: A device perspective on social media platforms and search engines. *Theory, Culture & Society*, 31(6), pp. 125–50.

2 The scientific and the subjective positions

Introduction

Network time is a social phenomenon. It is mechanical, computational and digital, but none of these dimensions removes it from the social realm, where it is instantiated and exerts its influence. This essential social character is captured in our conceptualisation of network time as something *lived* – it is an example of Barbara Adam's (1998) notion of a *timescape*, a *practised* time defined by its rhythms and tempos, particularly the sense of quickening that is perceived through near-simultaneous experiences. Consequently, network time is conceived as being *qualitatively different* from other types of time, slower mechanical rhythms, biological times and, perhaps a little confusingly, clock time, the hegemonic timescape of the industrial age (Hassan 2003, 2009, 2014).

This emphasis on the social dimensions of network time can be a little confusing because, as we discussed in the previous chapter, the phrase 'network time' is also used to describe the precise calibration of the clocks that oversee the synchronisation of computers and data networks. In other words, network time is also a highly quantified, mathematical phenomenon, even when we are focussed on its sociality. There is a clear tension in this dichotomy: how can a timescape be so closely measured and recorded yet also fluid, variable, even elusive? Is it simply the case that human beings are themselves poorly calibrated to network speeds, so that the timescapes feel chaotic and disorientating despite being highly regulated? Or is there something more fundamentally problematic with our sense of temporal separation? Does it make conceptual sense to separate social time from the computational devices that supposedly produce it, so our descriptions of the experience are completely alienated from the protocols that regulate it?

These are difficult questions that ask us to grapple not only with the complexities of the network, but also with our fundamental assumptions about time itself: what it is, where it comes from and how we experience it. The separation of temporal experiences from an abstract but universal mathematical time is almost as old as temporal theory itself, and it largely mirrors the division between the natural and the social sciences. In order to address this separation and to appreciate its implications for network time, it is helpful to review the long history of temporal theory. This will help us understand why such different ideas about time persist, allow us to assess both the validity and the usefulness of the separation, and suggest possibilities for reconciliation.

A brief history of time

It is important to note at the start that this brief history is limited, dealing entirely with Western science and philosophy and largely avoiding any discussion of Eastern, Middle Eastern and Indigenous philosophies, which have often demonstrated a far more nuanced engagement with time (Muecke 2004). There are a couple of reasons to limit the discussion in this way. The first is practicality. The history of Western temporal thought is still long and complex and it will be difficult enough to do it justice in a single chapter even without engaging with temporal theory from other cultures. The second reason is that the separation of subjective and objective times, which is the philosophical separation underlying the social and scientific categories, is itself largely rooted in Western theory. Other cultures have been far more receptive to specifically located conceptualisations of time and far less concerned with absolute and universal explanations of these local experiences. In Mayan, Incan and Indian philosophies, for instance, time is fundamentally a cyclical phenomenon:

> There is another measurement of time. Not Western time, but the time Indian philosopher Sarvepalli Radhakrishnan calls, ‘the great world rhythm. Vast periods of creation, maintenance and dissolution follow each other in endless succession.’ Wisdom is not in the future; it is in the return, the coming and going, the endless repetition.
>
> (Grant 2020: n.p.)

The idea of universal, linear and mathematical time arises in the Western tradition and occurred first to the Greeks, to whom we still look for inspiration and for the earliest iterations of our modern frameworks for knowing the world. In Greek thought, the question of time is intimately associated with the question of change and two oppositional positions that date back to Parmenides, for whom nothing changed, and Heraclitus, for whom everything was always in flux. These two positions are impossible to understand without some appreciation of the role played by religion in Western philosophy, and specifically the belief in an eternal, heavenly realm independent from the experience of humans on earth.

When Parmenides suggested that nothing changed, he was making a metaphysical argument about the relationship between human beings, their limited earthly experience and the exaltation of an eternal God. He is often credited with 'discovering' the category of timeless truths and for arguing for a monist belief in heaven as a singular unchanging reality (Hoy 2001; Sattler 2019). The everyday events and experiences that give sense and shape to time are therefore cast as illusory and time itself is not considered real. This superficial reading does not do justice to Parmenides's philosophy, but it is sufficient to establish the contours of difference between him and his predecessor, Heraclitus, for whom the backward-turning cycles of fire and water were the engines of perpetual flux (Russell 1946). Heraclitus is associated with the familiar axiom 'everything changes', which is supposedly derived from a metaphorical river that is both always the same (the river) and different (flowing water) for anyone who steps into it. Things both change and stay the same in a dialectical sense, and it is this unity of opposites that contours the experience of perpetual change.

It is worth emphasising again that neither Heraclitus nor Parmenides offers us a theory of time directly; rather, both propose a relationship between matter and being. They struggle with the apparent contradiction in a world that is defined empirically by both change and persistence, one that is simultaneously populated by both events and objects. This contradiction is important because it has proved challenging for time theory ever since, and Parmenidean and Heraclitan ideas are echoed even in modern-day attitudes to the *nature* of time. The two positions – one defined by flux and the other by stasis – reflect fundamental ontological uncertainty concerning the relationship between local experience and universal law. It was this same ontological uncertainty that concerned both Aristotle and Plato, who were similarly opposed in their theories of events and objects, and the relationship between them in time.

Aristotle and Plato outlined the foundational positions that have developed into the modern approaches to subjective and objective time. Aristotle focussed on events and the relations between events, and from this concern is derived the reductionist view of time. In this understanding, time does not exist outside or beyond the events that produce it. Plato focussed on the persistence of objects and proposed that time is a universal container for these objects – this container exists regardless of whether or not there are objects to fill it. This view is sometimes called 'absolutism' with respect to time. We can align it Parmenidean stasis because time is celestial and eternal; it defines a realm of heavenly or universal law, a perspective from which the events of humankind are momentary and incidental happenings (Emery et al. 2020; Rau 1953; von Leyden 1964).

It is possible to trace modern ideas about time back to the foundational positions of Aristotle and Plato because they have changed remarkably little in the years since, despite centuries of review, argument and supposed development. Indeed, one might wonder whether the apparent circularity of our temporal reasoning might have something to tell us about the subject of that reasoning. When Sir Isaac Newton proposed a universal mathematical time to frame his laws of motion, he made it external to and independent from human experience – a time only accessible to God. When Gottfried Leibniz argued with him that space and time were relative and not absolute, he was advocating for a relational positional that would later inspire Albert Einstein. The same disagreement about the nature of change continues and, by extension, the *location* of time remains uncertain (Emery et al. 2020). It is hardly surprising that so many books on time begin by quoting St Augustine: 'What then is time? If no one asks me, I know what it is. If I wish to explain it to him who asks, I do not know' (St Augustine 2002).

In order to understand the *modern* distinction between objective scientific time and subjective social time, it is necessary to revisit an argument at the beginning of the twentieth century, which involved the physicist Albert Einstein and the philosopher Henri Bergson, and again revolved around this question of absolutism versus reductionism. As the historian Jimena Canales (2015) has documented, the schisms of that period are highly implicated in the separation of temporal thought into distinct factions, which became more distinct as the twentieth century advanced.

Einstein had defined time through his theories of special and general relativity, first developing relativism into a formal theory of time dilation, then reconciling the variability of temporal experience with Newton's externalism via the concept of spacetime – a four-dimensional geometry that can bend with gravity. In special relativity, Einstein first dismantled the idea of a universal 'present time', a now, and proceeded to define time through motion relative to the speed of light, which is the sole universal constant. At very fast speeds – those that approach the speed of light – time begins to slow, so an object moving at those speeds literally experiences less time than an object in relative stasis. Einstein was able to prove mathematically that time could be simultaneously variable and predictable, provided it was treated as a product of relative motion. It is this principle that general relativity develops, adding time to the three dimensions of space to form an all-encompassing spacetime, a system of four dimensional coordinates that replaces Newtonian mathematical time as the orientating framework for all physical relations (Greene 2000; Rovelli 2018; Smolin 2013). Within spacetime, the independence of time becomes questionable. Einstein famously wrote that time was an illusion, and his Block Universe theory, which rests on the four-dimensional interpretation of spacetime, is widely accepted in physics and posits that past, present and future all exist simultaneously.

Einstein visited Paris in the spring of 1922 to debate time with the French philosopher Henri Bergson. Einstein argued for his conceptualisation of spacetime because it was the only interpretation of time that existed objectively, meaning that it be could be proven mathematically and revealed experimentally. Bergson, however, continued to insist that time was something different from this, despite the public consensus moving decisively in favour of Einstein. For Bergson, Einstein's mathematical description of relative motion simply did not capture the full complexity of the temporal experience. He did not deny the existence of spacetime, nor did he oppose the logic of Einstein's calculations (although he was sometimes accused of misunderstanding them), but instead argued that time involved another phenomenon that Einstein was not describing. To make this distinction, Bergson proposed that time (in the Einsteinian sense) should be differentiated from *durée* (duration), which he defined in personal-relational terms (Canales 2015).

The subtlety of the distinction that Bergson was making has often been overlooked in the years since 1922. In Bergson's view, duration was a culmination of thinking about time as experience. It echoed the psychology of William James (1901) in viewing time as something simultaneously *in the world* and something intimate and personal, deeply embedded in the sense of the individual subject.

While Einstein argued that time must be measurable, Bergson considered duration fundamentally impossible to measure. Indeed, it is the impossibility of measurement that defines the temporal phenomenon: quite simply, there is nothing continuous about the experience.

Central to the distinction between time and duration are Bergson's concepts of quantitative and qualitative multiplicities. In Bergson's view, Einstein could measure spacetime because it is categorically the same everywhere. It is what Bergson calls a quantitatively homogeneous multiplicity: one experience of spacetime is indistinguishable from every other experience of spacetime, and because they are of the same type they can be counted. Of course, this homogeneity is implicit in the act of quantification. We count continuous variables, which means every instance of that variable must be identifiable via a unifying and identifying property. Time expressed as duration is not like this. Temporal experiences are categorically different – they are qualitatively heterogeneous. As we transition from one temporal experience to the next, we notice this difference, which is largely how we interact with the sensation of time passing: duration is different from one moment to the next (Lawlor and Moulard-Leonard 2020). In Bergson's view, this discontinuity is fundamental to the conceptualisation of temporal experience. It is nonsensical to count time because time is defined by difference; its character simply cannot be described by numbers.

Recall from the previous chapter that the definition of network time stated it was a '*qualitatively* different form of time from its technological predecessor': clock time (Hassan 2009: 67). This emphasis on qualitative difference is directly traceable back to Bergson's distinction between different multiplicities. In this view, network time is more than clock time accelerated – it is a fundamentally different temporal category: the emphasis is firmly placed on the subject's *interactive experience* of this emergent form.

As the twentieth century progressed, Einstein's intuition and his maths were proved repeatedly by both argument and experiment, and Bergson's objections to the reductive limitations of spacetime were largely ignored. It wouldn't be quite accurate to say that they were forgotten, because the qualitative view of time was adopted, and indeed extended considerably by the phenomenology of Hegel and Heidegger, and later by the continental philosophers. However, in the popular discourse, in science, in business and industry, and across multiple domains of globalising social experience, the mathematical and universal view of time dominated. Of course, this dominance was closely associated with the clock and the regular intervals it provides for counting and costing time. The story of time in the twentieth century is largely a tale of regulation, synchronisation and increasing automation.

However, if Einstein's apparent 'victory' over Bergson had settled temporal matters decisively, then we would not be concerned about tensions or contradictions in the conceptualisation of network time. Indeed, we would not be concerned with network time at all, because neither special nor general relativity provides for its existence. In reality, temporal matters have not been settled decisively, not even within physics or science more broadly. Temporal questions continue to occupy both critical specialists and the public at large. The truth of the matter is that, faced with disorientating temporal experiences such as COVID-19, spacetime is not particularly useful. As Bergson discerned, there is something in our experience of time that is intimate, personal and poetic, something discrete to the individual subject that cannot be reconciled with a universal temporal block.

The science of time

Before we reflect on how social theory has developed to account for this subjective experience, it is worth considering some unresolved issues in the science of time, because these will become pertinent later when we look for similarities between the two approaches. The other 'grand theory' of twentieth-century physics is quantum mechanics, which was mostly developed during the first half of the twentieth century by luminaries such as Max Planck, Niels Bohr and others (Rovelli 2018). In a very simple sense, relativity theory operates on a grand, cosmic scale and quantum theory operates at the other end of the spectrum, concerning itself with individual particles of matter and energy. There is not sufficient space here to describe quantum theory in any detail, and I cannot do it justice, but there are a handful of ideas that can easily be grasped and that are very relevant to a discussion about time.

As the twentieth century progressed, physicists discovered that the universe behaves differently and unpredictably at the quantum level, in ways that seem incompatible with the 'macro' theories of motion and relativity. It is worth noting that both string theory and loop quantum gravity were developed to try to resolve this apparent incompatibility between the two grand theories. As yet, the project has not been successful. The implications for time are profound. Whereas Einstein's intervention sidelined the 'essential temporality' of time, quantum gravity confounds this temporality by making it variable, interactive and probabilistic. In other words, the assumptions that time is the same everywhere, that it is predictable and that it can be treated like a dimension of space seem a little less certain. So do some of our basic suppositions about the properties of time, including that it is directional, moving from the past, through the present and towards the future.

In effect, quantum mechanics destroys any remaining sense in science that time is universal and constant. Instead, it reimagines time as both discrete and local, the product of particular system-bound processes of 'becoming'. The word 'system' is used here as it is in physics, to mean an artificial but coherent (in some ways self-selecting) reference frame for analysis (Smolin 2013). There are a couple of important things to note about systems. First, everything can be considered as a system, including things that seems very much like objects. This is because nothing is static at the quantum scale: everything is always assembling or disassembling, as particles and forces interact momentarily. This means that objects – even objects that seem permanent – are always in flux, moving from one state to another. The author Carlo Rovelli (2018: 87–88) offers the following evocative description of how quantum mechanics reframes objects as systemic events:

> The difference between things and events is that things persist in time; events have a limited duration … in fact, even the things that are most 'thing-like' are nothing more than long events. The hardest stone, in the light of what we have learned … is in reality a complex vibration of quantum fields, a momentary interaction of forces, a process that for a brief moment manages to keep its shape, to hold itself in equilibrium before disintegrating again into dust.

The second thing that quantum mechanics tells us about systems is that they are indeterminate and interactive. Although we may choose to isolate a system in order to study it, this is a conceit. Systems are always being shaped by their interactions with other systems, and inevitably that dynamic includes us, the observers. Quantum theorists call this interactivity *super-positioning*, and it means that systems have some perplexing properties. For instance, it means a system is only 'fixed' into a particular state when we interact with it. At other times, we simply cannot be certain what sort of configuration it holds, so we must conclude that the system exists probabilistically, distributed across a 'cloud' of possible states. By far the most famous example of this phenomenon, of course, is Schrödinger's poor cat, which once inside its box is both alive *and* dead until someone thinks to check on it (Schrödinger 1935).

What are the implications of super-positioning for a physical theory of time? Foremost, it means that temporal measurement is always tied to the instrument doing the measurement, and that instrument is tied to a specific place and, crucially, a limited perspective within the wider field of systemic interaction. In other words, time *when measured* is not a universal phenomenon, but something *specific and local* to the act of measurement. This introduces a strand of phenomenological thinking into physics:

> the physically realizable states of a system have the same construction in both time and space. Any differences between space and time, such as dynamics and conservation laws, emerge phenomenologically.
>
> (Vaccaro 2018: 3)

Under such circumstances, the concept of a universal temporal experience begins to look very uncertain, especially when considered alongside Einstein's relativity arguments. We have noted already Einstein's suggestion that much of time is illusory, which is an idea related to the argument that, within the Block Universe, all times past, present and future are thought simultaneously present. Some physicists are prepared to go further, to deny the existence of time altogether and to suggest the universe is entirely static – there is neither time nor change:

> Space and time in their previous role as the stage of the world are redundant. There is no container. The world does not *contain* things, it *is* things. These things are Nows that, so to speak, hover in nothing.
>
> (Barbour 1999: 16)

These are not settled questions, though, and arguments about time – and certainly arguments that involve time – remain at the cutting edge of theoretical physics. While some physicists are prepared to remove time from explanatory theory, others seek to re-centre it, arguing that, far from being static, the universe is always being produced in time (Smolin 2019). These time-centric models emphasise specifically located histories: all matter revolves through an arc connecting its specific past to its specific future.

We should take away two main points from this summary discussion about the physics of time. The first is that even within the scientific model, which is the consensus approach across much of time studies and, more widely, across the different domains of social practice, there is still some uncertainty about what time is and how time functions. There are unresolved disputes between physicists, which exist not at the margins of the theory, but at the core of the ideas that predict mathematical and universal time. The second point is that tensions exposed by these debates, and the solutions that may possibly resolve them, suggest that time is a specifically located and interactive phenomenon. In other words, should a resolution ever be reached, it may well look somewhat similar to the Bergson-inspired social conceptualisation of time. Perhaps the deep bifurcation between scientific and social time studies is a good deal shallower than is commonly acknowledged.

Social time

In order to explore the depth of that difference, however, we must acknowledge that social time theory has also developed since Bergson, mostly in ways that have made time more fragmented, more subjective and more elusive. We covered some of the ideas central to social time theory in the previous chapter, when we defined and described network time, but it is worth considering these ideas in their wider context. Since Bergson, there have been some significant developments in how we conceptualise, locate and study instances of social time, and as a result of those developments I think it is fair to say that most social time theorists would consider nonsensical any argument for closer alignment with scientific time. If we wish to make such an argument, we will first have to convince social time theorists that we understand their arguments for social *difference* and that our new temporal model can speak to those arguments.

While Bergson's distinction between quantitative and qualitative multiplicities provides an important historical context for the current state of social time theory, it is not sufficient on its own to explain the approach that social theorists adopt in time research. We have already defined social time as being primarily interested in the comparative description of *timescapes*, or different patterns of social practice, with distinct rhythms and tempos. Yet it is not entirely clear what is fundamentally social about these rhythms, or what they can tell us about social action and social practice more broadly.

If we want to make sense of the role played by time in wider social theory, it will be necessary to reflect a little more closely on the distinctly social elements of social time theory. Bergson's clear distinction between scientific and social time foregrounds the relationships between human experience and 'time'. To understand the significance of that relationship, we must appreciate the influence of the psychologist William James (1901), who argued before Bergson that time was constructed in large part through our ability to perceive it. James defined 'the present', which he called the *specious present*, as a period of short duration that the human mind is able to hold in focus. The present moment, *being now*, emerges through human consciousness and the human brain's awareness of itself, being active in the world. This short duration could vary between a few seconds and a minute in James's estimation.

There are some obvious vagaries in this description that have prompted several authors to question forensically precisely what is being perceived in this variable present moment. Is it only events that we perceive? If that is the case, how do we compare delays between events, or arrange those events in order, determine sequence or differentiate between events happening virtually simultaneously? Several decades after James, Ernst Pöppel (1978: 714) defined five 'elementary time experiences', arguing that 'time perception has to be related to the occurrence of events as they are perceived and actions taken by the subject'. Duration is the perception of temporal space between events and the sense of time passing through that space. Duration is perhaps our most intuitive and familiar experience of perceptual time. It is variable – time can drag and it can fly – yet we standardise our units of duration: the seconds, minutes and hours that fill our days are all measures of duration.

In order to perceive duration, we must first perceive simultaneity – or, rather, the absence of simultaneity, which Pöppel calls succession. At very short durations, we seem to lose our ability to perceive events as separate. There is a 'minimum time interval that can separate two events so that they are perceived as non-simultaneous or successive' (Burdick 2017; Hirsh and Sherrick 1961). Once we can perceive events as not being simultaneous, we can perceive sequence or order, but again at very brief intervals (a few milliseconds) ordering can confuse us. Early work on reaction times suggested that somewhere between 5 milliseconds and 20 milliseconds might be a reasonable approximation of the duration of our temporal processing units (Eagleman 2008; Pöppel 1978).

The ordering of events in time makes possible the perception of tense – that is, the memory of events in the past and the anticipation of events in the future. In between these projected tenses is our perception of the present – or nowness, in Pöppel's terminology – which is similar to the 'specious present' and also called the 'subjective present' (Burdick 2017). Importantly, nowness has duration; it is not a disappearing line between past and future, but an arc of consciousness lasting perhaps just a few seconds. Future time is not perceived directly but rather anticipated. 'The temporal organization of future actions can be called anticipation or planning' (Pöppel 1978: 716) and, by definition, must surely involve introspection rather than the perception of external stimuli. As such, it is somewhat more complex for the perceptual empiricist to describe.

I am not certain that Pöppel's five time experiences on their own are sufficient to fully describe the human capacity to perceive time; the list may also be too long, complicating and confusing a more fundamental framework for interaction. In Pöppel's account, events are perceived, but these are momentary stimuli that themselves must have some sort of temporality, or duration at the very least. We should also note that describing the human capacity to perceive time does not itself explain time, or even describe time directly. Our temporal intuition tends to suggest that events happen *in time*, even if we are unconvinced by the necessity for an absolute and universal time-space. We assume that time would continue to happen even if we were not around to perceive it happening – or I think that most of us do – so what do we refer to as time in that scenario? What is it?

There is an argument that the question 'What is time?' makes little sense beyond our everyday practices of using time to order and translate our experiences. In this view, time *is* the abilities we have to perceive it and the habits we have to use it, and this can seem like quite a compelling explanation (Norton 2012). To my mind, though, it does not seem sufficient to locate time fully within the human capacity for event perception, nor does it seem sufficient to reduce it to everyday practice. If the former were the case, then surely we would see far more in the way of temporal variation, created by our psychological differences, and surely that sort of variation would have some sort of effect in the world. If time were fully a product of perception, then why does time appear to act in the same way on everyone? Why are there not more anomalies, humans able to slow time through slowing certain acts of perception? It seems intuitive that time is somehow independent of our psychological processes. If time is simply habit, then why does time so often feel like something being done *to* us? I think we feel the weight of time in ways that suggests the phenomenon is more complex. On occasion, time will feel heavy so that it drags and we are dragged down with it, or it may feel like it is floating and fleeting and we will sense its loss in the rush of it all. In my experience, the same events happening in the same order can prompt both sensations. Surely when we sense time we are doing more than perceive events as we are habituated to perceive them: we are perceiving events *in time*.

More philosophically, I don't believe that a list of time experiences, whether it is 5 or 50 items long, can fully describe the heterogeneity implicit in Bergson's notion of qualitative multiplicities. This is an idea that presupposes the impossibility of measurement, not the moderately difficult challenge of measurement. If time were simply a product of neuro-psychological capacity, of mental event-orientation, then it would be more easily quantifiable. The fact that it is not – or has not yet been so – suggests that social time theory must involve more than event perception and orientation. Perhaps the most forceful argument for this view is also one of the oldest (in terms of social time theory). It is found first in the philosophy of Husserl and Hegel, then more forcefully in that of Heidegger, and it is the idea that time is the coming into being of humans in the world all together.

It would be simplistic and a little misleading to suggest that Heidegger follows Hegel, who follows Bergson theoretically, not least because the chronology of that timeline is all wrong, but also because the history of temporal theory is no more linear and unitary than its subject matter. In Hegel's dialectical view of time and then in Heidegger's *Daesin*, time is an existential structure of human existence, an omnipresent denominator of human *becoming.* I associate these ideas with Bergson's *durée* because all grapple with the sense of time being something fundamental in the world of the human subject (McCumber 2011). Heidegger, in particular, goes further than Bergson in claiming time for phenomenology. In *Being and Time*, time is the coming into being of the world and the subject together. This is a difficult argument to unpack (and I don't plan to do so here), but it is important to note the crucial distinction that Heidegger is making. He rejects the idea that time is a universal 'flow' of now-points or events, as we have been calling them, and instead considers time to be the coming together, or the realisation, of past, present and future within the being of the human subject. The past and the future are held in tension, between memory and anticipation, and the present is the moment of self-actualisation – our opportunity to become ourselves (Heidegger 1967). This idea recalls the Greek concept of *Kairos*, the sense of the opportune moment, of meeting time where it finds us and where we find it (Hassan 2019).

It would be ludicrous to think that I could explain time in Heidegger within a single paragraph. These ideas are complex and challenging and, it should be said, not without fault. The point that I wish to emphasise is that phenomenological philosophy – largely a twentieth-century project – treats time in a way that is qualitatively different from its conceptualisation in Greek thought. It goes further than Bergson even, in that it fully internalises time into our being in the world; we are time, in a sense. Consequently, there can be no discussion and no analysis that does not foreground the human experience in the temporal framework. Bergson's distinction between two types of time is fully realised and radicalised. According to this view, the scientific model, which concerns itself with external events, only describes an incidental part of the temporal experience. However, Heidegger hardly suggests a clear, alternative analytical approach. The language of coming into being together can feel compelling but is fairly obtuse: What does time look like in this framework? How will we recognise it? If we assume that Bergson's description of *durée* is fundamentally the same type of time that Heidegger recognises, then we can say at least that time will be described qualitatively, but that still leaves us well short of a fully functioning social paradigm for time study.

What does a fully realised social time look like and how did it develop through the twentieth century? Central to the phenomenological concept of time is the idea that the world is realised through our awareness of it – the subject and the object are tied together in a mutually constitutive relationship. Implicit in this idea is that time is somehow related to another foundational concept in modern social theory: meaning. Following Max Weber, 'sociologists attempting to explain sociocultural objects [comprising] social actions need to understand the subjective meaning that the actor gives her/his own actions' (Tada 2018: 996). Meaning is the act of the subject interpreting the world, which in some sense is also the act of creating the world. It is a complex and problematic concept and our precise understanding of it will evolve as we move with the historical development of social time theory. For the phenomenologists at the turn of the century, and for the sociologists aligned with them, meaning (or Sinn following Husserl) is produced through this inner-subjective time or, conversely, time is the product of meaning-making. So, while central, time was 'too elusive a concept' (Nowotny 1992: 425) to compete with the measurable scientific alternative in the popular imagination.

I don't intend to suggest that the development of a specifically social time theory was a linear or narratively sequential process. Different ideas were formed at different times in different places, and emphasis shifted between different elements of the internalised human experience. We have already discussed the idea from the French sociologist Henri Lefebvre (1992) that time can be revealed to us through an analysis of its rhythms: time and space are interrelated in the experience of everyday life. Another Frenchman, Paul Virilio (1977), situated time within the accelerating logics of social transformation, particularly transformation realised through technological development. For Virilio, acceleration was the defining temporal dynamic of late-age modernity, a type of militarisation of the political-economy, as practices from hyper-fast warfare were adopted in various aspects of social governance and architectural planning. The logic is inescapable, hardwired almost into social forms and political institutions: 'Governance by speed (by states or otherwise) is logistics, and logistics, like the oceanic vectors from which it is born, is omnidirectional' (Bratton 2006: 12).

The language of theorists like Lefebvre and Virilio can be hard to grasp, making it difficult to discern exactly what dynamic or process or experience is being described. In Virilio's case, in particular, the adoption and adaptation (occasionally inconsistently) of temporal terms from physics – acceleration, velocity – has led to criticism that these theories of social time are confused about the phenomenon that they think they are describing (e.g. Sokal and Bricmont 1999). In confronting this criticism, it is important to remember that the phenomenon being described is not meant to align with its physical counterpart. We might even suggest that it would be logically inconsistent if velocity had exactly the same meaning in social and scientific time theory, because the times being described in both cases are different.

However, I think it is fair to say that the criticism of confused temporal terminology in postmodern time theory does identify an issue that we need to address. In seeking to describe the shape, form and sensation of subjective social time, theorists necessarily reach for language that we already use to describe time. Mostly that means borrowing and abstracting language from science. The terms that prompt criticism are the terms that we have in practice to describe the speeding up, slowing down or maintenance of relative motion. More fundamentally, in science the language of time is a product of speed: we are conditioned to think about time using these terms, and so when we talk about time we are invoking a framework of physical laws and mathematical equations, whether we mean to or not:

> Unless one learns to perceive human societies, living in a world of symbols of their own making, as emerging and developing within the larger non-human universe, one is unable to attack one of the most crucial aspects of the problem of time.
>
> (Nowotny 1992: 427)

Perhaps this is why a fully socialised theory of time struggled to develop relative to its scientific counterpart – it found it hard to differentiate itself and to articulate how social-temporal phenomena were real and actual and requiring explanation. On the surface, such struggles might lend support to Einstein's argument that being objective and empirically verifiable made spacetime the only definition worth pursuing. However, being on the surface, such a reading would also be superficial. Our ongoing struggle to describe a phenomenon might also speak to its complexity and our limited ability to recognise and decode that complexity. This, of course, is largely the argument that Bergson was making – heterogeneous multiplicities are difficult to describe from one instance to the next. They are variable, elusive and intuitive. The fact that we reach for the familiar language of (a more easily described) quantitative multiplicity says little about the qualitative multiplicity, but far more about our conceptual limitations.

Fully realised social descriptions of time were slow coming, but there were key breakthroughs in the latter part of the twentieth century, through which a more comprehensive understanding of the qualitative experience was slowly established. Increasingly, time was conceptualised as the relationship between different change-variables and the location (both material and symbolic) of those variables. Responding to his concern that we lacked a theory of the concept of time, the sociologist Norbert Elias (1993) defined time as a relationship rather than as a thing. He located social time in the relationship set between a subject and two continua of changes, one of which is treated as a standard continuum (such as the clock, for instance). This is a key development, I think, a crucial formalisation of qualitative thinking and a framing that is surprisingly contingent with the views of time emerging from the quantum sciences: 'Elias opens the way for grounding the concept of time again in social terms' (Nowotny 1992: 427). Questions remain about the relationship between specifically social times – that is, those created wholly within the world of symbols – and those of biological and cosmological origin, but we can leave them aside until the next chapter.

If we accept this framing, the challenge then becomes one of identifying and describing the different continua in which changes are happening. This is daunting challenge because, if it is a product of relationships, time can emerge in an infinite variety of forms, each of which will be difficult to describe qualitatively. Pluritemporalism is the idea that time exists in multiple varieties and that temporal study should therefore concentrate on describing the differences between variants. In many respects, the emergence of pluritemporalism explains the deep bifurcation that currently exists between social and scientific time theories: it 'allows for asserting the existence of social time next to physical (or biological) time without going into differences of emergence, constitution or epistemological status' (Nowotny 1992: 428–29).

I have always found this disinterest a problematic feature of pluritemporalism. As Nowotny (1992: 429) notes, 'By concentrating exclusively on upon "symbolic time", the dualism separating society – reflexive systems – from nature – non-reflexive systems – is not only unquestioningly accepted by social theory, but reasserted'. Furthermore, the decision results in the various limitations that we identified in Chapter 1 relating to the explanatory capabilities of social time and the absence of a comparative analytical framework.

What pluritemporalism does provide, however, is a rich and varied descriptive discourse, charting different social times for different peoples, practices and places. We have accounts of multiple types of work time, leisure time and familial time; timescape features for labour types as varied as academia and the production line (Hassan 2009; Pels 2003); complex descriptions of time in science (Pickering 1995) and in politics (Pond 2016); ethnographies of time in music studios (Marshall 2019) and analyses of multiple media times (Kaun et al. 2016; Weltevrede et al. 2014). In these accounts, social time is a deeply perspectival phenomenon derived from the events that bring social practices into being through specifically located social actions. In his social account of scientific time, James Pickering (1995) describes a 'mangle' of different practices and different rhythms that are twisted together by the production of scientific knowledge. Participant in these mangled rhythms are people, materials, technologies and ideas – they are assemblages 'at the same time natural, social and discourse' (Latour 1996: 369).

From these different accounts, we derive descriptions of the events that constitute different continua of changes, and we can identify repetitive patterns (rhythms) that give these continua shape and 'flavour'. However, we continue to lack an underlying temporal framework – a theory of the concept – to explain how these different rhythms relate to each other and to the human subjects caught in the mangle. Our descriptions are themselves abstract and elusive, and we forever run the risk of blurring concepts that elsewhere have narrow, more precise meanings. Is there anything that we can do to address this?

Systems of change

In Chapter 3, we will consider a framework that aims to provide specificity and structure to the relationships connecting fluid timescapes. This framework adopts Elias's 'triangular' relationship-set, in which a subject (most likely a human actor, but possibly a measuring instrument) engages with two continua of change – one a timescape under study and the other a standard continuum. The chapter seeks to develop this idea in respect to quantitative time study so that, in Chapter 4, we can discuss what an empirical toolkit might look like. Before that, however, we must review a couple of further developments in social time theory that develop our understanding of reflexive (social) and non-reflexive systems. Integrating these system types is absolutely necessary to advance the discussion.

First, let's try to be more precise about what Elias meant when he referred to 'continua of changes'. What counts as a change and what exactly is it that co-locates changes within a continua? What makes them continuous? What are the processes by which one set of changes relates to another? What are the relationships between these continua that supposedly produce time? These are ontological questions – they ask us to consider the fundamental interactions that constitute being and becoming in the world. They require a fundamental theoretical response. If there were more space, I would describe a range of possible theories that might serve the purpose. In particular, I would emphasise the potential of rhizomatic approaches such as assemblage theory (DeLanda 2006, 2016; Deleuze and Guattari 1980; Deleuze and Parnet 1977) and actor network theory (ANT) (Callon and Latour 1981; Latour 1987, 1999, 2004, 2011). These ideas share a commitment to the transitoriness of objects and the relational nature of becoming: 'the assemblage's only unity is that of a co-functioning: it is a symbiosis, a "sympathy". It is never filiations which are important, but alliances, alloys; these are not successions, lines of descent, but contagions, epidemics, the wind' (Deleuze and Parnet 1977: 69).

Both assemblage and actor network theory offer a compelling account of an emergent social reality, in which there is a continuous reordering of people and things material and symbolic. Both offer an expansive framework for locating Elias's change continua and both appear largely compatible with a social and quantum conceptualisation of pluritemporalism. However, in my view a more compelling and systematic account of relative change within social processes is found in the social systems theory of Niklas Luhmann (1990, 2016). In Luhmann's systems theory, we find both a macro-conceptual framework contiguous with assemblage theory and actor network theory, and a granular, event-specific account of what constitutes change within systems. It is this account, which Luhmann develops under the label *autopoiesis*, that allows us translate the abstract notion of relative change into detailed descriptions of system-specific processes.

In Luhmann's social theory, systems are self-selecting and self-differentiating, which means they define themselves as entities through constant comparison with their environment. Autopoiesis is this ongoing action of self-constituting comparison, the reassertion of difference between that which is the system and that which is not (Luhmann 1990; Schwanitz 1995): 'I thus begin with the claim that a system *is* difference – the difference between system and environment' (Luhmann 2016: 38). According to Luhmann, who is inspired here by the calculus of George Spencer Brown and the sociology of Gabriele Tarde, nothing ever happens without difference. The act of differentiation, the drawing of a line on a blank page, is necessary for the separation of self from other: it is the fundamental act upon which all existence is predicated. Systems are therefore complex operations for maintaining, reasserting and developing difference, and it is this logic that aligns the concept of systems with the 'continua of changes' that we are seeking for the production of social time. What is it that locates a continua and differentiates it from other continua? In systems theory, it is autopoiesis: the internal-external facing cycles of self-differentiation.

This statement leads to an obvious follow-up question: How does autopoiesis work? If we accept Elias's logic that changes within continua are the 'engines' producing time, then this directly implicates autopoietic operation – the changes we seek will be systemic acts of self-differentiation. According to Luhmann, systems are closed to each other and to their environment: 'On the level of its operations the autopoietic system does not receive any inputs from the environment but only perturbations (or irritations), which then might trigger internal operations in the system' (Seidl 2004: 3). Systems are therefore ideal candidates for locating change continua because they are both unitary and discrete: changes are always internal operations to the system. Comparing change sequences relative to each other is thus an act of organising systems, of pacing the internal operations of one system against another and a third standard continuum for reference.

Luhmann (1976: 135) defines time as the 'interpretation of reality with regard to the difference between past and future'. The act of interpretation is the act of self-differentiation:

> for Luhmann, consciousness and communication are not strictly speaking attributes of life but of systems; *meaning* and *life* are not attributable to each other … It follows that social systems are not based on individuals, their perceptions or even acts; they are constituted in communication … *Individuals use communication to reduce complexity by creating a boundary between themselves and the outside world, and they are constituted through their act of communication with that environment.*
>
> (Hartley and Potts 2014: 23–24, my emphasis)

Time production within systems is therefore dependent upon discrete meaning-making events, part of autopoiesis: *each event is an act of communication* that produces meaning and enables the internalisation of difference (Schwanitz 1995). This may sound familiar because it echoes the phenomenological framing that time is the production of meaning (*Sinn*):

> The meaningful unit of a system's element is neither a self-existing atom nor is it determined by something external; it is always defined as a system-internal choice through

> before-and-after relations in the present progressive process of operations, and through horizontal structures of the past and future (recollection and expectation), which are extensions correlated with the present ... To refer to the self is to refer to one's own temporality.
>
> (Tada 2018: 1001)

As far as Luhmann is concerned, a system does not self-differentiate *in time*; rather, time is something that 'the system continuously self-produces' (Tada 2018: 1004). For each system, then, time is being produced *subjectively* as the system differentiates between its past and its future, but time is also being produced *objectively* by other systems – by *all* systems, in fact – each with its own past and its own future. This view of time, in which it is both objectively and subjectively present and located within the becoming of specific entities, is a significant advance, I think, on the purely qualitative framing of pluritemporalism, because it engages directly with time's emergence, constitution and epistemological status. In other words, the systemic view of time allows for variability and qualitative local differences, and explains how those differences arise from specific self-differentiation processes.

The potency of this framing is evident when we reflect on how the systems model might inform some of the theories we discussed earlier in this chapter. With respect to the scientific approach to time, there is a clear sympathy between the quantum view of temporality in material systems, with its phenomenological implications, and the broader situating of time in Luhmann's social systems theory. In both cases, time is the product of event-orientated assemblage and system-bound – although, of course, there are different emphases in the definition of 'system' that direct our attention towards different types of event. In quantum theory, it is interactions between particles, waves and forces that matter; in social theory, it is the self-reflexive acts of meaning-making. In Chapter 3, we will ask whether these different event types can be aligned for the purposes of temporal analysis.

Similarly, if we relate system time to the 'pure' phenomenological theories of Heidegger and Husserl, we see the same emphasis on the realisation of self in relation to the world, and the location of time in the awareness of those twin dynamics unfolding together. Time, it seems, is always found in this curious relationship between internal and external rhythms, the subjective experience of self-in-the-world and the objective experience of the world-not-the-self. This is the same point that

Elias made when he located time in the relationship between the subject and two continua of change, one pacing the becoming of the world and the other acting as an external referent. If we can accept the fundamental alignment of these principles, I think this raises an important question for pluritemporalism. At the moment, the impossibility of measurement is predicated on the assumption that events within systems producing social time are fundamentally heterogeneous, which means they cannot be described by quantitative measures. In the systems view, however, these events are not fundamentally different – they are all internalised acts of self-differential meaning-making. Systems may well have different operations, different processes and different structures for coordinating this activity, but the fundamental action is the same. Something happens – an interaction, an event – and the system must interpret that happening in relation to itself and in relation to the world that it is not. The experience of difference arises from the relative experience of internal and external interpretation, the ratio of one change-continua compared with another.

In the next chapter, I ask what is possible if we fully accept Elias's assertion that a third continua can standardise this fluid relationship of relative differentiation. Could we begin to imagine a comparative empirical account of pluritemporalism? At the very least, could we standardise our toolkits for describing timescapes, so that our descriptions of social time are not wholly contextual?

References

Adam, B. (1998) *Timescapes of Modernity: The Environment and Invisible Hazards*. London: Routledge.

St Augustine (2002) *The Confessions of St Augustine*. Project Gutenberg. http://www.gutenberg.org/

Barbour, J. (1999) *The End of Time: The Next Revolution in Physics*. Oxford: Oxford University Press.

Bratton, B.H. (2006) Logistics of habitual circulation: A brief introduction to the 2006 edition of *Speed and Politics. Speed and Politics*. In P. Virilio (ed.), *Speed and Politics*, 2nd ed., trans M. Polizzotti. New York: Semiotext(e), pp. 7–25.

Burdick, A. (2017) *Why Time Flies: A Mostly Scientific Investigation*. New York: Simon & Schuster.

Callon, M. and Latour, B. (1981) Unscrewing the big Leviathan: How actors macro-structure reality and how sociologists help them to do so. In K. Knorr Cetina and A.V. Cicourel (eds), *Advances in Social Theory and Methodology*. London: Routledge, pp. 277–303.

Canales, J. (2015) *The Physicist and the Philosopher: Einstein, Bergson, and the Debate That Changed Our Understanding of Time*. Princeton, NJ: Princeton University Press.

DeLanda, M. (2006) *New Philosophy of Society: Assemblage Theory and Social Complexity*. London: Bloomsbury.

DeLanda, M. (2016) *Assemblage Theory*. Edinburgh: Edinburgh University Press.

Deleuze, G. and Guattari, F. (1980) *A Thousand Plateaus: Capitalism and Schizophrenia*. London: Continuum.

Deleuze, G. and Parnet, C. (1977) *Dialogues*. New York: Columbia University Press.

Eagleman, D.M. (2008) Human time perception and its illusions. *Current Opinion in Neurobiology*, 18, pp. 131–36.

Elias, N. (1993) *Time: An Essay*. Oxford: Blackwell.

Emery, N., Markosian, N. and Sullivan, M. (2020) Time. In N. Zalta Edward (ed.), *The Stanford Encyclopedia of Philosophy*. Stanford, CA: Stanford University. Available at: https://plato.stanford.edu/entries/time. Accessed 29 December 2020.

Grant, S. (2020) *On Identity*. Melbourne: Melbourne University Press.

Greene, B. (2000) *The Elegant Universe: Supertrings, Hidden Dimensions, and the Quest for the Ultimate Theory*. London: Vintage Books.

Hartley, J. and Potts, J. (2014) *Cultural Science: The Evolution of Meaningfulness*. London: Bloomsbury.

Hassan, R. (2003) Network time and the new knowledge epoch. *Time and Society*, 12, pp. 225–41.

Hassan, R. (2009) *Empires of Speed: Time and the Acceleration of Politics and Society*. Leiden: Brill.

Hassan, R. (2014) A temporalized internet. *The Political Economy of Communication*, 2, pp. 3–16.

Hassan, R. (2019) *Uncontained: Digital Disconnection and the Experience of Time*. Melbourne: Grattan Street Press.

Heidegger, M. (1967) *Being and Time*. Oxford: Blackwell.

Hirsh, I.J. and Sherrick, C.E. Jr (1961) Perceived order in different sense modalities. *Journal of Experimental Psychology*, 62, pp. 423–32.

Hoy, R.C. (2001) Parmenides' complete rejection of time. In L.N. Oaklander (ed.), *The Importance of Time: Proceedings of the Philosophy of Time Society, 1995–2000*. Dordrecht: Springer, pp. 105–29.

James, W. (1901) *The Principles of Psychology*. London: Macmillan.

Kaun, A., Fornäs, J. and Ericson, S. (2016) Media times: Mediating time – Temporalizing media. *International Journal of Communication*, 10, pp. 5206–212.

Latour, B. (1987) *Science in Action*. Cambridge, MA: Harvard University Press.

Latour, B. (1996) On actor-network theory: A few clarifications plus more than a few complications. *Soziale Welt*, 47, pp. 369–81.

Latour, B. (1999) On recalling ANT. *The Sociological Review*, 47(1), pp. 15–25.

Latour, B. (2004) On using ANT for studying information systems: A (somewhat) Socratic dialogue. In C. Avgerou, C. Ciborra and F. Land (eds), *The Social Study of Information and Communication Study*. Oxford: Oxford University Press, pp. 62–76.

Latour, B. (2011) Networks, societies, spheres: Reflections of an actor-network theorist. *International Journal of Communication*, 5, pp. 796–810.

Lawlor, L. and Moulard-Leonard, V. (2020) Henri Bergson. In N. Zalta Edward (ed.), *The Stanford Encyclopedia of Philosophy*. Stanford, CA: Stanford University. Available at: https://plato.stanford.edu/entries/bergson. Accessed 29 December 2020.

Lefebvre, H. (1992) *Rhythmanalysis: Space, Time and Everyday Life*. London: Bloomsbury.

Luhmann, N. (1976) The future cannot begin: Temporal structures in modern society. *Social Research*, 43, pp. 130–52.

Luhmann, N. (1990) *Essays on Self-Reference*. New York: Columbia University Press.

Luhmann, N. (2016) System as difference. *Organization*, 13, pp. 37–57.

Marshall, O. (2019) Jitter: Clocking as audible media. *International Journal of Communication*, 13, pp. 1846–62.

McCumber, J. (2011) *Time and Philosophy: A Histroy of Continental Thought*. Durham, NC: Acumen.

Muecke, S. (2004) *Ancient & Modern: Time, Culture and Indigenous Philosophy*. Sydney: UNSW Press.

Norton, J.D. (2012) What is time? Or, just what do philosophers of science do? Available at: https://www.pitt.edu/~jdnorton/Goodies/What_is_time/index.html. Accessed 29 December 2020.

Nowotny, H. (1992) Time and social theory: Towards a social theory of time. *Time & Society*, 1(3), pp. 421–54.

Pels, D. (2003) Unhastening science: Temporal demarcations in the 'social triangle'. *European Journal of Social Theory*, 6, pp. 209–31.

Pickering, A. (1995) *The Mangle of Practice: Time, Agency & Science*. Chicago, IL: University of Chicago Press.

Pond, P. (2016) Twitter time: A temporal analysis of tweet streams during televised political debate. *Television & New Media*, 17, pp. 142–58.

Pöppel, E. (1978) Time perception. In R. Held, H.W. Leibowitz and H.-L. Teuber (eds), *Perception*. Berlin, Heidelberg: Springer Berlin Heidelberg, pp. 713–29.

Rau, C. (1953) Theories of time in ancient philosophy. *The Philosophical Review*, 62, pp. 514–25.

Rovelli, C. (2018) *The Order of Time*. London: Allen Lane.

Russell, B. (1946) *History of Western Philosophy*. London: Routledge.

Sattler, B.M. (2019) Time and space in Plato's *Parmenides. Études Platoniciennes*, 15, pp. 1–33.

Schrödinger, E. (1935) Die gegenwärtige Situation in der Quantenmechanik. *Die Naturwissenschaften*, 23, pp. 807–12.
Schwanitz, D. (1995) Systems theory according to Niklas Luhmann: Its environment and conceptual strategies. *Cultural Critique*, 30, pp. 137–70.
Seidl, D. (2004) *Luhmann's Theory of Autopoietic Social Systems*. Munich: Munich School of Management.
Smolin, L. (2013) *Time Reborn: From the Crisis in Physics to the Future of the Universe*. New York: Penguin.
Smolin, L. (2019) *Einstein's Unfinished Revolution: The Search for What Lies Beyond the Quantum*. Harmondsworth: Penguin.
Sokal, A. and Bricmont, J. (1999) *Fashionable Nonsense: Postmodern Intellectuals' Abuse of Science*. New York: St Martins Press.
Tada, M. (2018) Time as sociology's basic concept: A perspective from Alfred Schutz's phenomenological sociology and Niklas Luhmann's social systems theory. *Time & Society*, 28, pp. 995–1012.
Vaccaro, J.A. (2018) The quantum theory of time, the Block Universe, and human experience. *Philosophical Transactions of the Roal Society A: Mathematical Physical and Engineering Sciences*, 376(2123), pp. 1–3.
Virilio, P. (1977) *Speed and Politics*. New York: Semiotext(e).
von Leyden, W. (1964) Time, number, and eternity in Plato and Aristotle. *The Philosophical Quarterly*, 14(54), pp. 35–52.
Weltevrede, E., Helmond, A. and Gerlitz, C. (2014) The politics of realtime: A device perspective on social media platforms and search engines. *Theory, Culture & Society*, 31(6), pp. 125–50.

3 Systems, interaction and perspective

Introduction

In this book, I am interested in the idea that there is just one thing in the world that we call time. That is not the consensus at the moment, of course. We have developed a deeply bifurcated view of time in which our dominant approaches to theory are almost entirely alien to each other. In seeking to understand how and why these different ideas developed, I want to ask whether an alternative view might be reasonable. Can time be both an objective, realist phenomenon *and* fundamental to our subjective experiences? This is the key question for a unified theory of time because time clearly seems to be different things to us. After all, we have been thinking and writing about time for a very long time and we have grown used to the language of time, even though that language is deeply contradictory. Simultaneously, we hold that time is acute and personal – it drags, flees, coils and constricts around us, all while it advances inevitably and indifferently towards the future (or the world's end).

Our relationship with time is difficult because we simultaneously hold these two very different ideas about it while insisting that these views make sense together. As a result, our temporal thinking can be quite disorientating. In periods like this one, when a pandemic is making us feel time acutely, we also feel out of sync with ourselves somehow – deeply anxious, as Heidegger (1967) would have it. The theoretical challenge of time becomes increasingly important because it ceases to be a purely theoretical concern. We feel it in our lived experiences. Our temporal uncertainty affects us socially, psychologically and politically. We should want to address it.

Time is a compelling subject precisely because it defies easy classification. In the previous chapter, I reviewed some of the different ideas about time that define the scientific and social approaches respectively. While I noted that there were significant and perhaps even irreconcilable differences between these two approaches, I also identified some similarities and wondered whether certain similarities were more pervasive and more consequential than is commonly acknowledged. This idle wondering meets an immediate problem, however: if I propose that time is fundamentally the same in both the scientific and social scenarios, why does it not seem the same? Furthermore, given that it does not seem the same, why should we treat it as though it were the same – why is this even something to which we should aspire? What have we to gain? The discussion risks becoming inescapably circular. I make a case that time makes us anxious and uncertain when we divide it into different categories, but our experience and the resilience of the two categories argue against any hope of reconciliation. How can we move beyond this confusion?

In this chapter, we will attempt a reconciliation of bifurcated time theory. First, we will assume that the similarities between the scientific and social approaches are sufficient to suggest a contiguous explanation of temporal reality. Next we will interrogate the consequences of that assumption, and ask what this social-scientific reality might look like. Under such circumstances, assuming that time is one thing in the world, we will ask: How is it being produced? If it is the same thing, why does it present so differently in different scenarios? After all, our new model should explain why our separate approaches to studying time have persisted for so long and seemed so irreconcilable. Finally, if we can answer these questions given the mechanisms of production we have described, we will return to our original assumption about a contiguous temporal reality. We will ask whether we have reason to continue with it – does it make sufficient sense still, and does it promise a resolution to our confusion? If it does, how might we start to gather evidence of this unitary time?

Scientific and subjective similarities

Before we proceed with these tasks, it is worth recapping on the similarities around which the scientific and subjective approaches to time theory might be more closely aligned. The discussion in the previous chapter was fairly wide-ranging, and we covered many different ideas from the long history of temporal study. Many of the ideas are complex, and shades of similarity exist in many places; it may help to clarify and to categorise these similarities so we can specify some principles for reconciliation.

In concluding Chapter 2, I focussed on the temporal similarities between autopoietic and quantum systems, both of which assume a world in which systems are constantly assembling. It is possible, though, to simplify considerably the language we use to discuss these conceptual similarities. Ideas like autopoiesis and assemblage, super positioning and granularity (the last two from quantum science) can be difficult for the uninitiated, and may work to deepen the sense of separation between the two theoretical domains. A key part of reconciliation will surely be finding a language that is mutually intelligible to practitioners from both domains. This is less a call for 'commonsense' language and logic – not least because some of our more profound realisations about time are complex and counter-intuitive – and more a request for a clear and comprehensive categorisation of shared concepts. That is my aim in this section.

First, we should acknowledge that, in their modern forms, both scientific and social time theories align around a reductionist model rather than an absolutist position. The consensus view in both approaches, irrespective of other differences, is that time is located within the happening of events. Neither science nor sociology seeks time as a thing external to the world of experience, and neither conceives of time without change. This is an important point because it acknowledges the widespread rejection of the Platonic and Newtonian positions, both of which imagine that there is a temporal framework that presupposes the existence of this world and may somehow be separable from it. Time is an event-based phenomenon, meaning that we must pursue it through the happening of events.

Of course, this raises an immediate question: What is an event? Social and scientific time theorists have disagreed over the type of happenings that produce time. Indeed, this disagreement is largely what contoured the debate between Einstein and Bergson after the physicist restricted time production to empirically quantifiable events only. One of the key challenges for the reconciliation project will be describing a set of time-producing events that make sense to both scientists and social theorists. This is a point to which we will return shortly. For now, let us say simply that an event must be a happening that registers somehow, somewhere in the world of experiences. In other words, an event is an empirical change in the order of things, a shift from one state to another.

This definition is sweeping enough to capture both scientific and social phenomena. The acceleration of a particle, a momentary interaction between forces, a change in the mood of a conscious subject and the redistribution of power within a complex network of social relations are all recognised as time producers. Indeed, anything that produces observable change in the universe is implicated in this definition. This is another important point, which we should acknowledge. The social and scientific approaches both recognise that the *observation of time is always implicated in its production*. In science, for instance, this is the key revelation of special relativity – an object is only ever in motion relative to another object. Likewise, quantum theory recognises the integral (and inescapable) relationship between an observer and the experiment under observation. In social time theory, pluritemporalism locates time always within the local experiences of the social actor.

This similarity has implications for our definition of an event. When we say that an event must register somehow in the world, our phrasing should be a little more specific: an event must register with a subject or a system capable of attending to its happening. This rephrasing emphasises the co-constitutive construction of reality and the idea that change only happens in relative terms. This is why relativity, the quantum model, assemblage and actor network theories, as well as Norbert Elias's (1993) temporal continua, all emphasise the ontological significance of relationships between events – these relationships are the key components, giving reality its shape and its order. Our second acknowledgement, then, is a recognition that there is a level (for want of a better word) at which scientific and social time can agree on their conceptualisation of an event. This level is foundational – that is, it presupposes the differences between quantitative and qualitative events that led Bergson to distinguish so clearly between time and *durée*. That distinction is based upon exactly how events are perceived by the observing subject; it does not deny either the observation or the happening.

We can say, then, that both scientific and social time theories agree that time is a relationship between event happenings and event observations. There is also considerable agreement about how those events are related to each other in the production of time. The disagreement mostly relates to how different types of event should be interpreted temporally. Where the social theorist argues that all events are temporally relevant, the scientist counters that only events that can be described empirically and quantitatively can contribute to a *meaningful* description of time.

Meaning and time

It is unsurprising that this is essentially a disagreement about what we should find meaningful because so much else in our social, political and scientific communities is litigated under these terms. However, these differences are not themselves essential – that is, the different emphases in scientific and social time theories do not reflect a fundamental ontological incompatibility. I believe that the worlds described by the two theories are contiguous as long as we accept an event-orientated model of physical and social becoming. This does not necessitate a significant shift in our current thinking in either domain. The process is already well underway in both the physical and social sciences, as the previous chapter established in its brief descriptions of phenomenological physics and rhizomatic philosophy.

In physics, for instance, there is already consensus that events are the elemental components of reality:

> The difference between things and events is that things persist in time; events have a limited duration … in fact, even the things that are most 'thing-like' are nothing more than long events. The hardest stone, in the light of what we have learned … is in reality a complex vibration of quantum fields, a momentary interaction of forces, a process that for a brief moment manages to keep its shape, to hold itself in equilibrium before disintegrating again into dust.
>
> (Rovelli 2018: 87–88)

In assemblage theory, there is an increasingly strong emphasis on event-relationships involving both natural and social entities:

> This theory was meant to apply to a wide variety of wholes constructed from heterogeneous parts. Entities ranging from atoms and molecules to biological organisms, species and ecosystems may be usefully treated as assemblages and therefore as entities that are products of historical processes. This implies, of course, that one uses the term 'historical' to include cosmological and evolutionary history, not only human history. Assemblage theory may also be applied to social entities, but the very fact that it cuts across the nature-culture divide is evidence of its realist credentials.
>
> (DeLanda 2016: 8)

The term 'entities' is used because often in assemblage theory it can be difficult to discern the objective status of the things subject to temporary association. Are they things, or events, or something else temporally aligned – as we noted in Chapter 2 – through 'contagions, epidemics, the wind' (Deleuze and Parnet 1977: 69)?

In Niklas Luhmann's (1976) social systems theory, these things are more clearly events, I think, because events are central to the empirical description of change within systems. According to Luhmann, a system is defined by its autopoietic processes of differentiation and replication. Autopoiesis involves repetitive acts of communication through which the system recognises itself as different from its environment:

> Individuals use communication to reduce complexity by creating a boundary between themselves and the outside world, and they are constituted through their *act* of communication with that environment. In doing so, they also construct the outside world through which they know themselves.
>
> (Hartley and Potts 2014: 24)

I would argue that communication is clearly event-based. It is a response to discreet external stimuli. A communication act is a reassignment of significance within a wider symbolic sign system – it is an event in an ongoing meaning-making process, through which a system differentiates itself: 'From the wild dance of events, there emerges an ordered pattern of expectations that serves as a means of orientation for the events. In systems theory, this concept is to be found in many variations' (Schwanitz 1995: 147). As noted elsewhere, 'systems produce meaning for themselves through communication acts that assign significance to specific "actualities" (events) in an environment of abundant possibilities' (Pond 2020: 95).

According to Luhmann, 'communication can be considered as the basic unit of observation for the assessment of the operations of the social system' (Mattheis 2012: 628). Autopoiesis is a process of communication through which a system produces meaning about itself in relation to the world it inhabits. In other words, systems are always observing events happening in the world and simultaneously interpreting those events through internalised rules for assigning them significance. Ultimately, the communicative continuum is granular – significance must continuously be reasserted in just the same way that the constituent forces within a stone must continue to interact with each other to prevent the stone from disintegrating. Precisely because they are constituted through communication, systems are event-orientated assemblages.

So we can say that science and social theory can be aligned around these models of event-based assemblage. The world is a product of event-based assemblage in physical, social and symbolic systems. We can develop this conceptualisation and imagine a vast interactive event-field reaching to the edges of the universe, incorporating all systems – physical and social – with every moment of reality always becoming. This is possibly a difficult idea to appreciate. It requires a rejection of familiar object-orientated philosophies in favour of a fluid, interactive and energetic model for understanding the world. It is a post-humanist philosophy in that it draws no fundamental or elemental distinction between physical, biological or social systems – all are potentially available for interaction with each other in the field. Systems may align for a while, change each other, or contribute to an assemblage greater than the sum of their parts. Human-centred systems are fully integrated into the wider interactive system dynamic.

Where is time in this formula? For Luhmann (1976: 135), time is the 'interpretation of reality with regard to the difference between past and future', which means it is located within autopoietic processes and the production of meaning. Of course, this is very similar to the conceptualisation of time in the sociology of Weber, Simmel and Husserl, among others, for whom time is aligned with 'subjective operation of meaning-giving (*Sinngebung*)' (Tada 2018: 997). As we have discussed, systems produce meaning through communication, specifically through acts of value assignment within a semiotic system, so time is found within the ordering of these communication acts. These are the events that produce time – the internal-external interactions between an autopoietic system and its surrounding life-world.

On the surface, this would appear to align time with consciousness – the awareness of self – or at the very least with subjectivity – the ability to differentiate self from other. Does such a formulation exclude non-conscious and material systems? I don't think it necessarily does. The simple truth is that other types of systems may produce meaning in ways that make very little sense to us. We cannot interpret for another system what is meaningful from its own peculiar perspective, because our judgements – our observations and our analysis – are always shaped by our own autopoietic assumptions. We assume that meaning must somehow be embedded within our own sense of consciousness because this is how we understand meaning for human beings. There is no reason, however, to think that meaning production must work in exactly the same way for all systems. In fact, given the vast array of difference and chaotic, interactive potential, this would be a remarkably unlikely scenario.

Consequently, we cannot use the human-centric definition of meaning to locate or to describe temporal events in other systems. What can we do instead? There are two options. Either we reserve time (i.e. time as a product of human meaning) for humans and for their social systems, and exclude from time any system that we do not think capable of subjectivity. This is a very limiting and conservative view to take though, a throwback to a Cartesian idea that separates thinking humans from the world in which we find ourselves. It also continues exactly the dualism that has separated the social from the scientific position – it distinguishes between a time for humans and a time for everything else. Alternatively, we can be radical and extend the concepts of meaning and meaning-production to include any system-specific interaction event. Some of those events will appear to leave the system largely unchanged (they will produce persistence), while others will result in disruption and possible disaggregation. Some events will be material, others will be biological, yet others will be social or symbolic. The key point is that meaningfulness is no longer a production of conscious communication. Instead, it is made in assemblage – the continuation for a moment longer of any system as a cohesive, self-referential analytical unit:

> The meaningful unit of a system's element is neither a self-existing atom nor is it determined by something external; it is always defined as a system-internal choice through before-and-after relations in the present progressive process of operations, and through horizontal structures of the past and future (recollection and expectation), which are extensions correlated with the present … To refer to the self is to refer to one's own temporality. (Tada 2018: 1001)

This, I think, is our most cohesive, most radical and potentially most productive time theory, which could serve to reconcile the scientific and the social positions. Time is something that all systems are always self-producing as they maintain themselves as something different in a universal interaction field. Whether we are dealing with physical or social systems, the same type of process is happening.

The universal interaction field

What does the world of universal interactive assemblage look like? The answer to this question depends very much on where one is standing. There is no one way to describe the interaction field because, by definition, it will always be experienced locally. The universal system exists only in the sense that it is the sum of all the interactions between all the other systems. We can theorise its existence – we may even be able to model some of its behaviour – but experientially it only exists for the omnipotent. This idea may seem familiar because it follows a similar logic to that which led Newton to hypothesise *t*, his abstract, universal and mathematical time fully available only to God:

> The complex world of meaning is itself atemporal and chaotic, because all possibilities simultaneously exist there, with equal probability to be actualized. If one were an omnipotent observer (like God), one could actualize all such possibilities at once: This describes the eternal space in which all are simultaneously com-*present*.
>
> (Tada 2018: 1004)

No system located within the field has total access to all the interactions happening across it. Therefore, describing the universal interaction field is a challenge similar to the one that produced relativity theory. What are the constants that define experience when the world is always in relative motion around us? Newton thought time might play this role but Einstein, following Rømer and Maxwell, demonstrated the error in this solution, proving instead that it was only lightspeed that remained constant everywhere. Everything else – all matter – either sped up or slowed down depending on the relationships that defined its measurement.

In our model, motion is an example of a more fundamental interactive dynamic between systems. Certainly, systems can move relative to each other, but there are myriad other ways in which they can interact, all underwritten by communicative self-differentiation. After all, what does it mean for two systems to 'move' in relation to each other? It means that they are repositioned in spacetime, one advancing while the other retreats, or vice versa, depending upon the perspective. Students of introductory relativity theory may have read examples about spacemen drifting past each other in an otherwise blank void. In such circumstances, neither spaceman can tell whether one or both are moving, who is advancing and who is retreating, because the perception of movement is entirely dependent on their shifting perspectives. Movement depends on our ability to perceive it. We can use physics to model the arc of a spaceman through a series of spacetime coordinates, but that movement is meaningless without something else that can attend to it happening.

This is the crucial point: *external-systemic* change is always interpreted through an *internal-systemic* process that assigns meaning to stimuli differentially. Let's think a little more about the two spacemen drifting past each other. In the physical model, as I have just described it, the spacemen move and they attend to each other's movement, but that is it; they are otherwise non-entities, dumb objects with no internal mechanisms for making meaning. We know that spacemen are not like this. I have argued that almost nothing is like this. Perhaps elementary particles differentiate themselves only in space, but as soon as a system has any complexity it perpetuates in multiple dimensions. Autopoiesis is a process of meaning-making, but it is also a process of meaning-synthesis – the *synchronous interpretation* of multiple stimuli towards the assemblage of the overarching system.

The point I am trying to make here is that movement is only one element in a far more complex dynamic of self-differentiation and realisation. Even movement must be interpreted, and it is this interpretation that makes the interaction field *sensible for the systems within it*. As we have established, interpretation happens within systems through autopoiesis, so the inner life of the system is centrally implicated in the system's behaviour and its experience of the interaction field. In other words, the principles of relativity extend to all differentiation in the interaction field – or rather, we should say that the principles of differentiation in the interaction field extend to special relativity, which is particularly concerned with physical descriptions of energy and motion.

This realisation creates enormous complexity and presents a significant challenge for anyone hoping to describe the interaction field empirically. In response to the earlier question, we must say that what the interaction field looks like depends on where one is standing, the direction in which one is looking and one's own capacity to make meaning from these observations. Empirically, our experience of the interaction field is always limited by our capacity to observe and make sense of it.

We know this intuitively when we think about time. Let's return to our two spacemen drifting around in the otherwise blank void.

Each spaceman can only see one thing: the other spaceman. There are no other stimuli, nothing else in the world *to be experienced*, so the spacemen only have each other and their lonely thoughts. It's this second bit that is important, because, of course, spacemen have inner lives – a world of conscious reflection, of dialogue between the liminal and subliminal selves (Lewis 2008). In the physical model, we assume that this internal dialogue is the same for both spacemen, but in reality we know that this will not be the case. The two spacemen will have been shaped by different experiences, have different things troubling them, will talk to themselves in different voices with different cadences.

Imagine for a moment that one spaceman 'thinks' at half the rate of the other (Figure 3.1). Perhaps this spaceman had a sedative before entering the void, or perhaps he is practised in meditation, or perhaps there is no reason other than random chance, but it means that his thoughts are produced at roughly half the speed of his counterpart's thoughts. The result is that the spaceman is only able to register half of his counterpart's relative movement. When two spacemen have different internal response rates, they experience the same external events differently. In Figure 3.1, both spacemen float towards each other at the same speed for the same ten-second period. However, spaceman 1 on the left attends to the journey far more regularly than spaceman 2 on the right. In effect, he experiences twice as much travel as spaceman 2 does: his journey 'persists' through ten events, whereas for spaceman 2, the journey persists for five events. The temporal experience of this difference will depend on how many internal-facing events fill the periods in between these external happenings.

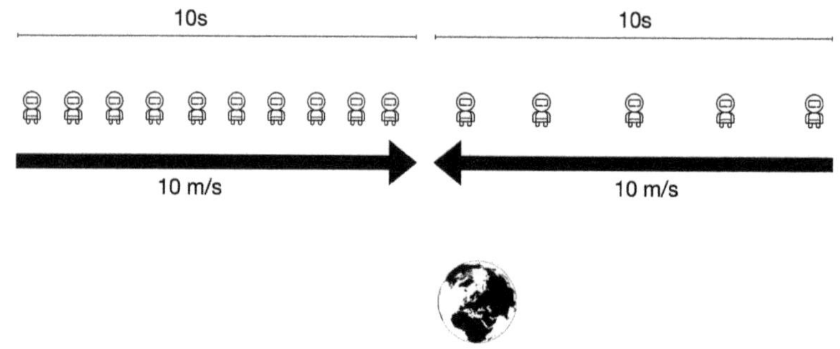

Figure 3.1 Spacemen in relative motion with different rates of thought

This relationship seems simple enough, but only because we are presupposing a temporal and spatial framework to make sense of the spacemen's relative speeds of movement and thought. This is a Kantian approach, adopting time and space as *a priori* frameworks through which to interpret reality. Such an approach seems sensible, but it is entirely dependent on the preconditions with which I began the example: the two spacemen are moving at identical speeds for identical periods. In Newtonian terms, I insisted upon a 'true' motion as a precondition of relative motion. What is it that defines these speeds, or the period of movement? There is nothing else in the void, nothing within which we can locate the 'rules' for relative movement, so we are forced back towards an externalising philosophy in which time and space write the rules for a universe while never fully appearing within it.

What if I hadn't set those preconditions and the spacemen were moving in their empty universe without any orientating information to help them (or us) make sense of that movement? In such a scenario, the second spaceman's slower rate of internal sense-making becomes something far more profound. We can no longer assume that his five observations represent neat two-second and 20-metre increments because there is no external framework to support that assumption. Instead, the spaceman's only way to make sense of a new observation is to relate it to his previous observations, through memory and through his internal processes for making sense of those memories. In other words, we have moved into a scenario in which the spaceman's internal differentiation is a key component of the external reality that he is experiencing. If we extend the logic of this discrete example to the entire interaction field, then we discover some peculiar and uncertain properties. Foremost among these is the realisation that the universe is a product of our capacity to experience it, which is an idea that should also sound familiar, because it is an important component of quantum theory, and we discussed it in Chapter 2.

I think it is important to recap a couple of points here. The first is that we have defined time as the ordering of autopoietic events through which all systems assemble. This means that time is produced by interactions *between* systems and by interactions *within* systems. Of course, interactions within systems are also interactions between systems, because all systems (including spacemen) are assemblages of component sub-systems. A human being is a product of interactions between chemical and biological systems, as well as symbolic and psychological systems, and interacts, in turn, with larger scale social and ecological systems. Systemic interaction is always happening across a multitude of scales and time is located everywhere in this dynamic. The second important point to recall is that, because time is the ordering of assembling reality, *all discussions about assemblage are temporal discussions.* When we discuss the relative motion of spacemen, we are using motion as a proximal concept to make sense of the underlying ordering of assemblage. That underlying order is time: it underwrites everything.

Perception and reality

Consequently, these efforts to understand the shape and the behaviour of the interaction field are efforts to understand time, especially given that our observations are always a partial and co-constitutive experience. This is an important realisation but not a new one. It occurred a hundred years ago to philosophers including Alfred North Whitehead and George Herbert Mead, as they grappled with the implications of Einstein's theory of relativity (Canales 2015). The problem that concerned Whitehead, Mead and others was how to proceed empirically in a world defined scientifically by relativity theory and intuitively by subjective perception. Whitehead (1934: 65) wrote that science 'is the issue of a coordinated effort, sustained for more than three centuries, to understand those activities of Nature by reason of which the transitions of sense-perception occur'.

In broad terms, Whitehead (1934: 26) was following Bergson and objecting to the scientific insistence in the reduction of knowledge to numbers, which produces theoretical explanations that 'are right as far as they go. But they omit … our intuitive modes of understanding'. The full complexity of Whitehead's response is well beyond the scope of our present discussion, but there are a couple of important points that I wish to note. The first is that Whitehead pioneered a response to the intuitive critique of science predicated on the theories of science. In other words, much like his contemporary and correspondent Bertrand Russell, Whitehead pursued a philosophy that was compatible with twentieth-century science but also critical of it. He sought to develop a scientific epistemology to account for intuitive experiences of reality where those experiences were also grounded in scientific logics. Whereas science, in receiving relativity theory, decided that it was unconcerned with human understanding of this mathematical reality, Whitehead argued that human understanding was more than relevant – it was co-constitutive. If we ignore subject intuition, which Whitehead defined as perceptual data on causal relatedness, we ignore half the evidence we have about the world. In effect, 'neither physical Nature nor life can be understood unless we fuse them together as essential factors in the composition of "really real" things whose interconnections and individual characters constitute the universe' (Whitehead 1934: 25):

> According to Whitehead, taking into account the whole of our perception instead of only pure sense perception … implies also taking into account the other half of the evidence, namely, our intuitions of the relatedness of nature, of 'the togetherness of things'.
>
> (Desmet and Irvine 2018)

To make his case, Whitehead called on the electromagnetic theory of James Maxwell, which emphasises the interrelatedness of forces within the universe. In Whitehead's view, electromagnetism defines the universe as a field of interactive forces, meaning that all things are in some sense *connected* forcefully together. There can be no isolation or abstraction in such a dynamic, no pretence that how we perceive the nature of things is immaterial to the true nature.

Perhaps it is already clear that many of the arguments made so far in this book are echoes of Whitehead's case that it is problematic to maintain a deep bifurcation in our knowledge about the sensory and material world. Moreover, in using electromagnetism to make the case for the causal connectedness of perception and reality, Whitehead was pre-empting arguments that would be made later by quantum mechanics. The argument being made here is also based on an interactive systems theory. Reality is defined by relations between things – particularly relations between experiences – and those relations extend to all things in the universe, in some way connecting them. Human experience is not exclusive within this dynamic.

Within that broad conceptualisation are specific consequences for a theory of time, which Whitehead perceived as being a phenomenon of discrete durations (quanta). What is particularly relevant for our current discussion is that time is similarly subject to Whitehead's insistence that natural and perceptual phenomenon should not be separated. Accordingly:

> Nature is in process, a process of becoming and a process of perishing. The emphasis is on the fleeting and temporally fragile nature of things … A theory of temporality must be an integral part of a dynamic theory of Nature.
>
> (Hughen 1985: 95)

Consequently, while Whitehead begins his temporal theory with a human-orientated account of perception – of durations much as Bergson and James understood them – he ends it 'with a comprehensive and dynamic theory of Nature' (Hughen 1985: 100). In between is a sophisticated effort to grapple with both mathematical and sensory reality.

Whitehead was not alone in his early advocacy for a reconciliation of the mathematical and subjective positions. As I have mentioned already, the response to relativity theory was energetic and global – the provocations that Einstein made were felt keenly and widely. Whitehead's ideas were also influential, and that influence can be identified in the physics of Percy Bridgman (1949) and the perspectivism of George Herbert Mead (Aboulafia 2008).

Bridgman is notable for many reasons, his Nobel Prize being one of them and his efforts to develop the field of operationalism another, but his argument contra Einstein that the world could not be *wholly relativistic* is most relevant here. Like Whitehead, Bridgman was prepared to insist that our experience of reality should be integral to our efforts to understand reality – it was insufficient to claim that mathematical truth existed independent of our ability to perceive it. For Bridgman, an entirely relativistic universe, in which our position within it is irrelevant, made little sense; instead, it was 'an obvious structure of experience' that measurement added validity to one perspective relative to others (Bridgman 1949: 354). We can frame this argument in phenomenological terms too, I think: the world takes shape around us and through us – and so who we are, where we are, and how we 'measure' really do matter.

The significance of 'perspective' is developed more fully in the philosophy of George Herbert Mead, who was Whitehead's contemporary and 'made repeated attempts to assimilate Whiteheadian concerns and concepts into his own evolving thought' (Cook 1979: 107). Mead's concerns were also far wider than the scope of this discussion, but I think we can frame his perspectivism as a contribution to the same argument for connection that Whitehead made between intuitive experience and mathematical Nature. For Mead, the defining characteristic of a subject's experience of its environment is its *limited capacity* to interact with it – all experiences are limited by the subject's limited perspective. This is the same regardless of the 'type' of subject, whether it is a simple organism, a human being or a technologically complex measuring instrument.

According to Mead, a universal and objective reality surely existed, exactly as Einstein and mathematical physicists argued, but it could only ever be experienced locally. He called these local experiences perspectives, so that perspective becomes the defining characteristic of objective empiricism. If it were possible to account for and to sum all the different perspectives within the universe, then the objective world could be fully revealed, but there are as many perspectives as there are 'quanta' of spacetime – it is an infinitely impossible challenge. In some respects, then, Mead is reversing Whitehead's reasoning that leads from intuition to Nature, and explaining how a subjective experience of the world can emerge from a universal objective reality. 'For Mead, for whom the totality of perspectives is the objective world, albeit one which offers no access without interpretation, it is the shared, intersubjective practice in which all temporal structuration emerges' (Nowotny 1992: 428):

> Perspectives involve contact and interaction between organisms and their environments. For example, a fish living in a certain pond can be thought of as inhabiting an ecosystem. The way in which it navigates the pond, finds food to eat, captures its food, etc., can be spoken of as the fish's perspective on the pond, and it is objective, that is, its interactions are not a matter of the subjective perceptions of the fish. Its interactions in its environment shape and give form to its perspective, which is different from the snail's perspective, although it lives in the same waters.
>
> (Aboulafia 2008)

In this framing, perspective is a positional construct, but it is also a temporal one. Reality is dependent upon both *where and when* a subject directs its attention within the interaction field. We have to decide exactly what this means. Do we think that 'when' in this framing is just another dimension of spacetime and therefore accept the simultaneous presence of all possible 'whens' within the

Block Universe? Or do we think that the act of attention brings possibilities into existence, which seems to make sense intuitively but leaves reality unresolved when our attention is elsewhere? Finally, we have to decide whether these questions are fundamental to the reconciliation of scientific and subjective time or if they can be located fully within the domain of theoretical physics. As students of human experiences within the interaction field, does it matter much what happens in our absence?

In response to the final question, I would suggest that it certainly matters – or at least that it should matter because human-centrism has long been a misleading influence on our social theory, often through exceptionalism. Moreover, any attempt to grapple with time as a realist phenomenon should engage with temporal possibilities in the absence of humans, not least because this will force us to consider more fully the complex implications of perspective within the interaction field. Both Whitehead and Mead argue that that we should reject this bifurcation between intuition and nature. If we follow that logic, then we should be thinking about time in the absence of humans precisely because doing so will inform our understanding of how human experience and time relate to each other. According to Mead, subjectivity is a positional construct, an effect of limited temporal-spatial experience within the 'multitude or plurality of temporal-spatial relations' (Nowotny 1992: 436). So what does this mean in terms of interactionist mechanics? What is the universal phenomenon, what is the local phenomenon – and do relations between these two phenomena produce such different and confounding time experiences?

History is local, the future is everywhere

One possible conclusion from Block Universe theory is that time is an illusion – or at least that the passing of time, sometimes called time's arrow, is an illusion (Price 2010). Proponents of this view argue that because all times are simultaneously present, the sense of temporal flow, of movement from the past, through the present and towards the future, must therefore be a product of our (limited) perceptual capacities. We often assume that Einstein held this view. In 1955 he wrote a letter to the grieving family of his friend Michael Bessos, which included the famous assertion that, 'People like us who believe in physics know that the distinction between past, present and future is only a stubbornly persistent illusion' (quoted in Conway 2016: n.p.). These days, the idea that temporal order is illusory is probably the consensus view among theoretical physicists (e.g. Rovelli 2018). According to the theory, the universe is a network of events onto which 'we project sequences of past, present and future' (Jaffe 2018). In other words, the sense of temporal order is an anthropomorphic problem, a mistake in our intuition – time is not *real* in the interactive universe.

While this may be the consensus view in physics, it is not universally accepted, and it is quite possible to find respected and influential voices for an alternative view: that time is both real and fundamental in the physical universe (Norton 2018; Smolin 2013, 2019). I don't intend to summarise or even try to explain these arguments here because I will not do them justice. It suffices to say that the question of the reality of time is not yet resolved within the physical sciences, and we have already discussed at length the problem of temporal realism in subjective time studies. The question I want to ask here is: What are the implications of perspectivism for temporal realism? Perspectivism is meant to move us away from ontological anthropomorphism, and to connect intuition and nature more coherently. What can it tell us about time?

In my reading of perspectivism, the significant realisation concerning time is that time is not an illusion of human intuition but rather a fundamental feature of specifically located perspectives. In other words, time is the real and necessary function of ordering and explaining the relations between different perspectives within the interaction field. Consequently, we reject the idea that time is a 'mistake' in human intuition because the same mistake is surely being made by every system – every single perspective – differentiating within the interaction field. There is nothing illusory about this: time is real because time is the relational ordering of difference (and, by extension, of differentiation events). Difference is real and foundational for all systemic action. 'Perspective does not mean that there is no objective reality but it does mean that objective reality is always experienced locally, which creates the impression of subjectivity' (Pond 2020: 114). It is this impression of subjectivity that leads physicists to claim that time is illusory, but this ignores the conclusion that localised experience is common to all systems. This is not something unique to conscious human beings.

We can think of this in slightly different terms. What is time? What are its attributes and what are its behaviours in our ontological models of the universe? We have a working definition from the previous chapter that aligns both the social and the scientific approaches to time with relationships between continua of changes.

In addition, we have now located those relations within a universal interaction field, in which changes are always acts of self-differentiation within locally specific systems. For those individual systems, it absolutely does make sense to speak of temporal order in realist terms. Every system has its history: it is on an arc of becoming, differentiating from what it was, into and through its current state. That history is the relational account of relevant events. Every system retains material and symbolic traces of the systems that it has met and the systems that have made it. Similarly, every system is balanced at the point of action in autopoiesis, translating between self and non-self. Systemic 'presence' is the act of communication, the moment of self-realisation in which the system locates itself in respect to the wider interaction field.

History and action are local because meaning is always made locally. This is the fundamental assertion of perspectivism. Objective reality is universal, so we can think of the future distributed in diffuse probabilistic clouds throughout this space, but this is a theoretical abstraction – it will only ever be realised locally. Time is only ever experienced locally by 'autonomous observers, or subjects, *sui generis*, who respectively cognize the world from their own perspectives' (Tada 2018: 1002).

Consequently, time is simultaneously a universal mathematical phenomenon and a local intuitive phenomenon, meaning that both the scientific and the social approaches are justified to the extent of their limited concerns. It is also true that both are only partial accounts, coherent and mutually sensible perhaps, but limited in the many ways we have discussed. Where does this leave the temporal reconciliation project? We have shown that the two approaches are not contradictory and that the separation of qualitative and quantitative experience is less fundamental than is sometimes assumed. An event-based, systems-orientated ontology can explain both our objective reasoning and our subjective intuitions concerning time because perspective always limits local experience of a universal phenomenon.

The next steps for the project are reasonably clear. First, we should propose a limited but specific definition of time that acknowledges its subjective-objective character. I suggest the following: *time is the relative differentiation between specific interactive systems*. This definition is not perfect, certainly, but it captures the dynamics of change-continua and locates those changes within the defined autopoietic process. This has the considerable advantage of suggesting to us the type of events we should be seeking *when we identify a system for temporal study*. With this definition in place, we can start to consider its implications for empirical time study. Somehow we will have to account for perspectivism, given its centrality to this temporal model. This will be a considerable challenge – the implications of perspective are complex, and many of the more confounding characteristics of time arise precisely because of the way a limited perspective befuddles our observations.

Perspective and the interaction field

According to our working definition, time is located in the interactive relations between (at least) two systems and its production is a function of the perspective of those two systems. Additionally, because we are seeking ways to observe and measure time, our own perspective matters. In other words, we must also consider our limited capacity as observers to attend to the interactive relations between our study systems, and we need some way to account for how our limitations are shaping our observations. The discussion of interactive time study is always confusing in this way: there are so many moving parts, so many conditional statements and estimations of actuality, that it can quickly become overwhelming.

In Chapter 4, I will explore in detail the challenges of time measurement given the interactive differentiation theory I have described in this chapter. Almost all those challenges arise because systemic interaction is such a complex and variable dynamic. To conclude this chapter, then, I wish to introduce the basic principles with which we will approach these challenges, and to explain how they are grounded in theory. Let's begin with a statement of these basic principles and ensure that the statement is as simple as it can be. Our aim is to establish whether or not repeatable empirical observations are possible. If they are, we can then proceed to the challenges of quantification and measurement.

According to the systems-theoretical view that time is *relative differentiation*, three dynamics are happening simultaneously that combine to produce time in the world:

- First, there is the universal-objective phenomenon of *systemic interaction*, which incorporates both the internal differentiation processes of individual systems and the communication-initiating interactions between different systems. These interactions together constitute the universal interaction field, the fabric of event-based reality, and are the engine of time.

When we speak of time as the ordering of events, these are the events: all events are acts of systemic differentiation.

- Second, there is the phenomenon of *perspective*, which limits any system's capacity to interact in the universal field. Perspective is why it is a little too simplistic to conflate time wholly with interaction – time is interaction, acknowledging the influence of perspective in realising that interaction. Very shortly, we will spend a little more time on this second dynamic, because it is both crucial to our conceptualisation of time and also very confusing.
- Third, and finally, the relationship between subject and the interaction field is relational and relativistic, meaning it is shaped by *the ratio of self-differentiations* between the observer and observing perspectives. This dynamic will be our primary focus in Chapter 4 because it is central to the challenge of measurement. It acknowledges that the 'inner time' of an observer is a key component in the construction of 'outer time' in the world. We touched on these ideas briefly in our discussion of spacemen and relative motion.

In order to study time empirically, we must address each of these dynamics both conceptually and methodologically. The overarching challenge is that we must observe system-specific differentiation events, both internal and external, simultaneously for implicated systems and then synthesise these events in a way that captures the complex dynamics of interaction between the systems. The task is made more complicated still because our act of observation – our method of recording – is also system-dependent. This is a consequence of the second dynamic described above: time is a product of perspective. The issue is that perspective is a far more challenging phenomenon than we have considered so far. Those challenges become more evident as soon as one tries to engage with perspective experimentally. Our task – assessing the possibility of measurement – will depend largely on our ability to rationalise the implications of perspective for empirical observation.

For instance, we know that the act of observation itself is implicated in the systemic assemblages that we observe. This is a subtle point, and can sound confusing, but it flows from the behaviour of systems at the quantum scale and we discussed it briefly in the previous chapter. The act of observation 'fixes' a systemic assemblage in the moment of observation, but this does not logically imply that the systemic assemblage is always in the state in which it is observed. This interactive dynamic, which implicates the observer in any experimental record, is one of the fundamental assertions of quantum theory.

Similarly, in phenomenological theory, the 'observer' (more commonly, the human subject) is implicated in bringing the world into being through her interaction with it (including the action of observation). The implications for the 'un-observed' world are uncertain, although – if we recall the quantum approach – we can assume that it exists in a probabilistic 'cloud' of possibilities, which at least allows us to model its possible behaviour. The implications for the observed world are more complex still. While we confirm its existence through our act of observation, we must simultaneously accept that it continues to exist probabilistically – alternatives may be possible if only we were observing differently.

All inter-system interaction is a function of perspective – that is, the system's awareness of its place and its (inter)action in the wider systemic universe. This dynamic is not limited to the act of observation; it applies to all interactions between systems. In other words, a system has to attend to an event happening (through autopoiesis) in order for that event *to be meaningful* and, by extension, for it to produce time. Consequently, just as our own perspective limits our capacity to observe interaction between study systems, so too perspective limits the meaningful interaction between the study systems. This means that we cannot simply estimate the time produced in an interaction between two systems simply by comparing linear event sequences for each system: the dynamic is more complex than this. We also need some way to estimate another system's perspective on the events that it is experiencing.

Simultaneously, we must decide whether the interactions that we observe are a 'true' representation of the interactions that would happen if we were not there to observe them. Relatedly, we must also consider how our own differentiation processes might be influencing the events that we observe. What would happen, for instance, if we were to change the calendar time of our study, making observations only in the morning rather than distributed throughout the day? What would happen if we changed our methods for identifying interaction events? Would we discover an entirely new domain of systemic connection somehow missing from our initial assessment? More formally, we can say that we must consider our own interactions with all three change-continua engaged in the production of time:

1 the study system (S_1)
2 the control system (S_2)
3 the observer (S_o).

What is particularly challenging about this relationship is that all three systems are, by definition, continua of changes, and changes within one system can influence the interactive relationship between all the other systems. No matter what we do, 'changes in the system may shape our ability to observe the system … the system itself can change how it presents to us' (Pond 2020: 117). Furthermore:

> to make any observations at all, the researcher cannot escape time. An observation requires action; it demands that the observing system is able to assemble and to make meaning, and that means that something within the system has to change, which binds it in time. If both the observing and the observed systems are in stasis, neither can change, and there can be no interaction: nothing happens. This is a crucial point, which follows inevitably from social system theory. An observing system must self-differentiate in order to observe; otherwise it cannot recognise or process new information.
>
> (Pond 2020: 117)

The consequence of all this relative movement is that we can never be wholly certain of the observations we are making – we can never *know* without doubt that the systemic configuration we observe is the same systemic configuration that would happen if we were not observing it. The best we can do under these circumstances is to make some assumptions about the probability that we what we observe is a true representation, and be ready to update those assumptions should the evidence we collect suggest it is necessary. This is the principle of establishing *priors*, which will be familiar to anyone who has studied or practised probability modelling. We will deal with the mathematics of these priors in the next chapter, but this is not a book on Bayesian statistics, so the discussion will be limited. Our aim here is to establish the principles of how this modelling can work, and to question their empirical significance.

Our first prior will establish the validity of Percy Bridgman's assertion that measurement elevates one perspective above all others – which is another way of saying that, despite there being multiple possible realities, the one we experience is the most probably actual:

> Our first assumption, then, is that this is indeed an obvious structure of experience and that therefore the configuration we observe is the most probable 'true' configuration of the system-set: S1,2a = S1,2.
>
> (Pond 2020: 122)

Making the assumption that the changes we observe are the same changes that would happen if we were not observing does not preclude the possibility of alternative configurations; it simply says that they are less likely. We can describe our assumption in more formal probabilistic terms. Imagine if we could take multiple observations of the same interaction events from multiple different perspectives. In theory, if the act of observation is implicated in the observed configuration, then multiple observations from multiple perspectives should reveal a more complete 'range' of configurations to us. Now imagine that we plotted those configurations to see whether some were being produced more often than others. We might assume that this is indeed the case, and that the range of possible configuration is distributed in some statistically describable way. Indeed, this would seem a perfectly logical assumption because the interactions between S_1 and S_2 are subject to the same autopoietic processes each time. It would be genuinely surprising if there were no order or pattern to how those interactions produced systemic meaning – such disorder would make the persistence of coherent systems incredibly unlikely.

When we assume that $S_{12o} = S_{12}$, we assume that the configurations are normally distributed around the observation S_{12o} – that is all. However, there is one further caveat. Earlier I suggested that this assumption was a 'prior', which would imply that it can be updated and improved through repetitive testing. Is this really true? I don't feel wholly confident giving an answer to this question, although I suspect that it can be true – but not in quite the sense that Bayesian modelling usually assumes. The problem with priors and the study of time is that time is always being produced in the moment of observation. If we repeat an observation, then by definition it is a different instance of time production, so it cannot inform our initial observation – or our prior – in an obvious or linear way. Even the previous discussion, in which I proposed multiple observations being taken from multiple perspectives, falls foul of this logic. According to the various theoretical principles that we have established, these are not multiple perspectives on the same temporal configuration, but rather different instances in which the temporal configuration is created anew each time. When we propose that $S_{12o} = S_{12}$, we are not proposing that S_{12} is a true configuration towards which we are making estimates; rather, we are making an assertion about the repetitive actions of time. In this assertion, we are claiming that, despite always being local, despite being a product of change, time is (re)produced rhythmically because of the autopoietic precedents through which systems reassert their internal coherence. This is a highly significant point. If we identify significant variation in the temporal analysis of a systemic configuration, then this implies that the autopoietic processes of the observed systems are changing rapidly relative to each other. Temporal study thus becomes a powerful indicator of systemic instability.

The key thing to remember during this discussion is that perspective is a relational construct. So far, we have considered how the empirics of the observed systems might hide or distort more complex interactive probabilities. Yet this is only half the challenge if we want to establish the possibility of empirical measurement, because our actions as observers also contribute to the dynamic. We have not ignored this possibility. We have just recognised that multiple or repeat observations of interaction between S_1 and S_2 would not necessarily reduce probabilistic uncertainty because the act of observation is itself a temporal construct. I did relate this point to change within the two study systems, but how can we be certain that the observing system (S_o) is not changing itself? What can we do to control for the internal differentiation – the inherent unreliability – of the observer?

Clearly there are various ways in which the perspective of the observer can change, and we have outlined some of these already. An observer can move in physical spacetime, for instance – an action that may bring some events into focus while obscuring others. We also discussed how the rate of internal differentiation may affect a subject's ability to observe relative movement. A path through spacetime is revealed differently to observers with different capacities to register those changing coordinates. There are many more ways, however, that the internal differentiation of an observing subject can influence the act of observation. After all, the 'act of observation' translates into a set of relations between two system-sets: S_o and S_{12}. We have established that changes within S_{12} will shape those relations, but it is equally logical that changes within S_o will have a similar effect.

There is not space here to try to describe the many ways in which an observer and its observations interact to construct variable, time-dependent perspectives. Obviously, that dynamic is itself hugely complex, and a multitude of different ways exist in which the relations between an observing and the act of observation can change. Therefore, it may be more productive to ask whether there is a way for an observer to try and limit the variability of their observations – to ask, when it comes to time study, whether it is possible to be scientific.

This question is our primary concern in the first part of Chapter 4. I attempt a critical temporalisation of the scientific method, by which I mean the standardisation of empirical observation. Of course, I acknowledge that this is a massively complex topic, and my contribution is limited to a couple of issues. First, I ask how we identify the different ways in which the *affordances* of our observational methods are shaping the phenomenon that we seek to observe. The act of observation is the relational interface between our internal and external worlds, so the question demands that we consider this relationship and establish how our internal differentiation – our capacities and our choices – may be shaping the interface. Second, I ask what we can do to control our internal differentiation or, alternatively, adjust for its influence. Science has various answers to this question, of course, and the scientific method can offer us guidance, but the challenge here is realising the full complexity of making observations *in time*. How do these continua of relative change challenge the scientific method, and what can we do in response?

References

Aboulafia, M. (2008) George Herbert Mead. In N. Zalta Edward (ed.), *The Stanford Encyclopedia of Philosophy*. Stanford, CA: Stanford University. Available at: https://plato.stanford.edu/entries/mead. Accessed 29 December 2020.

Bridgman, P. (1949) Einstein's theories and the operational point of view. In P.A. Schilpp (ed.), *Albert Einstein: Philosopher-Scientist: The Library of Living Philosophers*. La Salle, IL: Open Court, pp. 333–54.

Canales, J. (2015) *The Physicist and the Philosopher: Einstein, Bergson, and the Debate That Changed Our Understanding of Time*. Princeton, NJ: Princeton University Press.

Conway, D.J. (2016) *Time Is an Illusion: A Step on the Bridge*. Bloomington, IN: Xlibris.

Cook, G.A. (1979) Whitehead's influence on the thought of G.H. Mead. *Transactions of the Charles S. Peirce Society*, 15, pp. 107–31.

DeLanda, M. (2016) *Assemblage Theory*. Edinburgh: Edinburgh University Press.

Deleuze, G. and Parnet, C. (1977) *Dialogues*. New York: Columbia University Press.

Desmet, R. and Irvine, A.D. (2018) Alfred North Whitehead. N. Zalta Edward (ed.), *The Stanford Encyclopedia of Philosophy*. Stanford, CA: Stanford University. Available at: https://stanford.library.sydney.edu.au/archives/fall2018/entries/whitehead. Accessed 29 December 2020.

Elias, N. (1993) *Time: An Essay*. Oxford: Blackwell.

Hartley, J. and Potts, J. (2014) *Cultural Science: The Evolution of Meaningfulness*. London: Bloomsbury.

Heidegger, M. (1967) *Being and Time*. Oxford: Blackwell.

Hughen, R. (1985) Whitehead's epochal theory of time. *Philosophical Topics*, 13, pp. 95–101.

Jaffe, A. (2018) The illusion of time. *Nature*, 556, pp. 304–05.

Lewis, J. (2008) *Cultural Studies: The Basics*. London: Sage.

Luhmann, N. (1976) The future cannot begin: Temporal structures in modern society. *Social Research*, 43, pp. 130–52.

Mattheis, C. (2012) The system theory of Niklas Luhmann and the constitutionalization of world society. *Goettingen Journal of International Law*, 4, pp. 625–47.

Norton, J.D. (2018) Time really passes. Humana.Mente: *Journal of Philosophical Studies*, 4, pp. 23–34.

Nowotny, H. (1992) Time and social theory: Towards a social theory of time. *Time & Society*, 1(3), pp. 421–54.

Pond, P. (2020) *Complexity, Digital Media and Post Truth Politics: A Theory of Interactive Systems*. Cham: Palgrave Macmillan.

Price, H. (2010) *Time's Arrow and Archimedes' Point: New Directions for the Physics of Time*. Oxford: Oxford University Press.

Rovelli, C. (2018) *The Order of Time*. London: Allen Lane.

Schwanitz, D. (1995) Systems theory according to Niklas Luhmann: Its environment and conceptual strategies. *Cultural Critique*, 30, pp. 137–70.

Smolin, L. (2013) *Time Reborn: From the Crisis in Physics to the Future of the Universe*. New York: Penguin.

Smolin, L. (2019) *Einstein's Unfinished Revolution: The Search for What Lies Beyond the Quantum*. Harmondsworth: Penguin.

Tada, M. (2018) Time as sociology's basic concept: A perspective from Alfred Schutz's phenomenological sociology and Niklas Luhmann's social systems theory. *Time & Society*, 28, pp. 995–1012.

Whitehead, A.N. (1934) *Nature and Life*. Chicago, IL: University of Chicago Press.

4 Time recoded, time recorded

Introduction

At the end of the previous chapter, I said I would attempt a critical temporalisation of the scientific method. This is quite a difficult phrase, so I will begin this chapter by trying to spell out clearly what I think the challenge is and then how I want to respond to it. My aim is to formalise the various theoretical arguments that I have been considering into a framework for studying network time (the social concept) *scientifically* – that is, empirically and mathematically. After all, that is the challenge underwriting this project: is it possible to locate and to describe time in a way that makes sense to both social theorists and to scientists? In response to this challenge, we can socialise the clock or we can standardise our approach to the intuitive time experience. Ideally, we should do both. I think it is admirable and desirable to approach time as scientifically as possible, for reasons that I have already discussed, but I don't necessarily think that science – especially in its broader practice – has resolved its relationship with time particularly well. How often in the reporting of timestamped data, for instance, does science engage with interactivity or with the perspectival nature of time?

Initially, before we can hope to standardise or quantify the observation of social time, we need to address critically the role played by time in the scientific method. To my mind, this requires two things. First, we need to stop timestamping data without acknowledging that this is both a reductive and a social act (the issue here is that the clock is only one of the three change continua that interactively produce time); and second, we need to formalise the role that interactionism and perspective play in our measurement of time.

We have discussed this first requirement already, but only briefly. Researchers have attempted to measure network time – in Chapter 1, I described various time-series analyses of publication rates on different platforms, efforts to quantify 'patterns of pace' and even attempts to measure variability within platform-specific time production. All these efforts, however, ultimately locate events using timestamps, and thus tie time to the clock, presupposing the linear and universal advance of regular and predictable periods (t). Clearly this is problematic as far as the pluritemporal social time theorist is concerned; however, while it isn't exactly contradictory to the scientific understanding of time, it isn't entirely coherent with it either. Both relativity and quantum theory recognise the influence of perspective on the production and the experience of time – that is, they recognise that there is no singular universal time, an experience that is the same for everyone. Admittedly, as far as relativity is concerned, variation is tied to movement through spacetime, but quantum theory acknowledges that interactivity shapes time in other ways. Follow this logic, and the idea that there is a singular experience of network time for everyone, using a platform begins to seem fairly nonsensical. The notion of platform 'use' captures (and conflates) an enormous range of interactivity: users who 'work' on a platform professionally; users who are deeply invested in its culture and discourse; users who have structured and periodic interactions with the platform; and users who are only ever tangentially aware of it. The 'temporality' of the platform is surely different in these different scenarios.

This is arguably the main reason why simply timestamping events is inappropriate for estimating network time, despite the clock's presumed latency within the scientific method. What does 'presumed latency' mean? It means that time is not generally considered to be a variable within scientific experimentation – scientists set up experiments, change the proportions of reactants or modify their interventions, then record the outcomes at regular or predetermined intervals, and do not worry about the role the intervals themselves are playing in the outcome. In other words, science assumes that the outcome is the same both *inside* and *outside* of time. Generally, we report the result of an experiment without caveating it with a perspectival disclaimer – rarely do we say, 'This is result X but only for observer Y at coordinates Z'.

We cannot do this in an experiment designed to capture network time because we simultaneously ignore the perspectival complexity of the time phenomenon and confuse time as both something inside and outside of itself. This is why the quantification of social time has to begin with the deconstruction of quantification itself – we must first ask what we are trying to measure and which measurement tools we are planning to use. In the previous chapter, I described what it is that I think we are trying to measure (the relative differentiation of change-continua or systems); now it is time to address how that measurement should take place. What will be our method and what tools do we require?

The quantification of differentiation

According to the definition advanced in the previous chapter, *time is relative differentiation between interactive systems* – this is time as dynamic perspectival interactionism or T-RDIS for those who prefer Dr Who inspired acronyms. This definition means that there are three different dynamics that we must account for when we try to observe the production of time. First, there is the interaction between systems (S_1 and S_2), which will be an event-based phenomenon. Second, there are the relative perspectives of both the interacting systems *and* the perspective of a third observing system (S_o), all of which will contribute to the temporal phenomenon observed. Third, there is a relationship between internal and external differentiation processes that is potentially different for all three systems, a product of the external events being experienced (the stimuli) and the internal mechanisms for making sense of those events (autopoiesis).

These three dynamics create multiple challenges for the empirical study of network time. First, we must somehow identify and locate events that signify interaction between systems, recognising that not all events will involve direct material engagement *and* that there will be different categories of event defined by the external and internal differentiation relationships of the different systems. Second, both the shared and the distinct event sets are situated relative to each other in a relational structure that is both dynamic and perspectival. Rather than 'fixing' the relations between systems for the purpose of our observations, we will require some way to describe the *change* that is happening – this is what time is, after all. Third, we need some way to deal with the communicative dynamic that is so central to time. Recall that systems theory regards all events as communication acts because each time something happens in the world, it must be processed by the sense-making apparatus of an autopoietic system. When we refer to the relationship between internal and external differentiation, we acknowledge that everything that happens in the world is ultimately interpreted by locally situated systems. Somehow, then, when we try to describe network time, we need to capture the reality that network time – though created across a system-set in our definition – is always realised *locally* (and possibly differently) in the sense-making of each system.

Taken together, these various challenges constitute another argument against the linear tracking of network time-series. In my experience, as soon as one tries to describe network time in this way, it soon becomes clear that important dynamics are being overlooked. In my first analytical engagement with network time during my doctoral research, I realised that my efforts to describe time on Twitter were foundering because 'Twitter time is a complex assemblage of relative flows *in different structural and textual layers*' (Pond 2016: 289, my emphasis). In other words, any description of network time is always a description of multiple network times coming together through the act of observation.

The perspectival dynamic is particularly complex in this respect, as we also discussed in the previous chapter, because one of the weird quantum effects of perspectivism is that reality becomes probabilistic – we can never be sure that the phenomenon we observe is the same as the phenomenon that exists without our observation. I proposed that we circumvent this complexity, at least initially, by proposing that reality is normally distributed, and that we adopt the prior that our initial observation is *most likely* a 'true' representation of reality. This assumption is contiguous with Percy Bridgman's argument that measurement elevates one perspective above all others. This is a helpful step for the empiricist, perhaps – at least for our confidence in our capacity to observe – but it doesn't much help us with the perspectival uncertainty within the relationship between S_1 and S_2, nor does it help us standardise perspectives within the fluid interaction field. In other words, while we may be confident in the validity of our own observations, we cannot assume that the same observations would be made from another perspective – another user of the platform, for instance. Once again, the complexity of network time is that it is multifaceted – the sum of multiple, individual, temporal experiences.

How should we deal with this complex uncertainty? The first thing to realise is that we do not have to start from scratch. Many of these difficulties are the same ones with which theorists have been wrestling since the separation of subjective and objective more than a hundred years ago. The significance of perspective did not occur to George Herbert Mead (1938) in a vacuum – it was recognised and described in the foundational theories of relativity.

In fact, in case it is not already obvious, special relativity theory's primary aim is to describe the motion of objects from the perspective of objects that are themselves in motion. The Lorentz transforms, which describe the relationship between two observers moving relative to each other (like the spacemen in the previous chapter), are a pair of equations, *each of which is defined by a positional expression*. According to these equations, a mathematical description of the experience of time is only possible if the relative positions of the two observers are available. In other words, there can be no relativistic description of time without there also being a description of the positional relationship of the observers experiencing that time.

$$t' = \gamma(t - vx / c^2)$$

$$x' = \gamma(t - vt)$$

The effect of the Lorentz equations is to transform the motion of an object so that it acts as though it were *not moving* relative to the other object. This is like saying (if I am one of the objects) that I can describe the movement of the other object as long as I can assume that I am not moving myself. Can we attempt something similar to simplify the relative experience of network time? Might it be possible to transform or 'lock' the temporality of the component systems, so that we can observe with confidence the time produced by each, in turn?

Personally, I am not convinced that this is possible. The significant hurdle we face is that we are dealing with perspectival dynamics that are far more complex than those transformed in the above equations. Relativity theory deals only with motion through spacetime – perspective can be described because it is simply a function of positional coordinates in that spacetime. For us, however, perspective is a function of position as well as the internal and external differentiation processes of different systems: 'Something that should be objectively identical can have different meanings for each subject, because of the different eigentimes (Eigenzeiten) subjects have respectively built by themselves' (Tada 2018: 1000). Additionally, perspective is embedded within complex networks of relations within the interaction field. It is shaped by learning and by culture, and a multitude of situating dynamics that defy quantification (Bergson 1999; Hall 1996; Lewis 2008). I cannot imagine an equation or an algorithm sufficiently complex to capture or to transform these dynamics. Indeed, as we have discussed already, the logic of the interaction field means that it would inevitably be trying to describe *everything* and we will have strayed well into metaphysical speculation.

However, our goal here is significantly less ambitious – we are not trying to describe network time *in its totality*. That is, we are not seeking t_{nt} because we have already decided that the pursuit of Newtonian time leads to hypothetical abstractions that deny the experience of time in the world. Instead, we are trying to describe our local experience of network time as best we can, meaning that our descriptions are objectively real, repeatable and comprehensible to other observers also experiencing network time.

We can achieve this provided that we accept that the measurement of network time has to begin with the self-differentiating system – it has to be rooted in the *subjective* experience. If we want to generalise that local-subjective experience, then we can do so additively (according to Mead), provided we can resolve the complicating dynamics of perspective. The key idea I want to propose and to develop in this section is that resolution is possible because perspective is itself a function of the differentiation process. By this I mean that an empirical description of the *distribution of perspectives across the system-set* is a product of the relative internal and external differentiation processes of each component system. In other words, we can estimate perspective if we can 'measure' the attention a system allocates to a set of interactions as a fraction of the system's total capacity for attention. For each system, if we can describe the fraction of total systemic attention dedicated to a specific set of time-producing interactions, then we can describe key elements of the subjective-temporal experience produced through those interactions.

Figure 4.1 depicts a Twitter network centred on the account of Donald Trump. Every node in the network has mentioned Trump by name and the large dot at the centre of the network is Trump himself. The coloured section of the graph shows retweet relationships between Trump and the different accounts that have mentioned him. In other words, these are the accounts with which Trump has interacted, retweeting their messages to his many millions of followers. While most observers of Trump's Twitter might reasonably assume that he devotes huge amounts of his time and attention to the website, the graph illustrates that he only attends to a small fraction of the interaction events that (potentially) involve him.

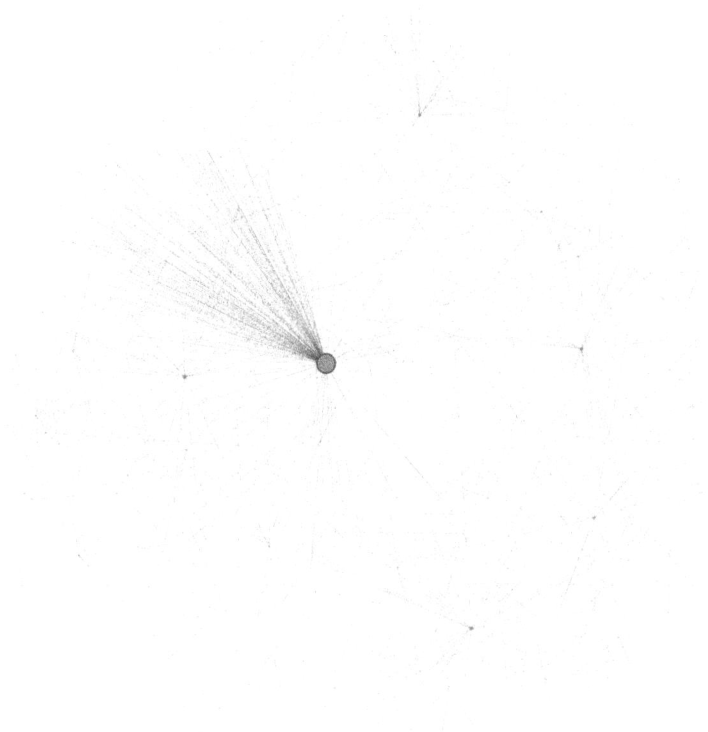

Figure 4.1 Twitter network centred on the account of Donald Trump

This is a rather confusing idea, so it is worth taking some time to spell out exactly what it means and what its implications might be. Perspective is obviously a massively complex phenomenon: it is multi-variable, as we established in the earlier chapter. It is constructed internally within a subject, in the interactions between a subject and its environment but also through networks of complexity in the interaction field. A full engagement with perspective surely requires high-level complexity theory, some sort of engagement with chaos and the uncertain probabilities that inevitably flow from these dynamics. In short, attempting to 'calculate' a full sum of perspectival complexity leads us back towards the impossibility of 'total system knowledge'. Instead, though, we can attempt to describe important dynamics within the perspectival relationships happening between systems producing time. It should be possible to estimate with some reliability how much of its 'total attention capacity' a system is paying to the processes that interest us.

One way to think about this is to consider one type of problem we encounter whenever we try to estimate network time. Imagine that we are interested in the temporal experience being created by a breaking news event on Twitter. As I write this, it is 12 hours since Donald Trump was diagnosed with COVID-19 – it feels like my attention is being sucked away from the world and wasted in this blank space of interminable, uninformative Twitter updates. It is very easy to send a query to Twitter and retrieve a sample of the tweets being published on this topic and to plot a time-series analysis of those updates, noting when they spike and when they fall, and how they measure against other topics also in the news. What is far harder, however, is to interpret the meaning of that time-series for any given Twitter user because, of course, for every user the experience of that time-series is dependent upon their engagement with those tweets. It will vary depending on their use of the platform, the accounts they follow and myriad other variables, many of which we can only guess at (many Twitter users will be following the Trump story, but not all of them will also be trying to write a book about time). In short, their engagement with the Twitter temporality of the Trump diagnosis is entirely dependent on how much of their attention they allocate to it.

However, if we can estimate their interaction with Trump-Twitter as a fraction of a wider interaction set, then we can start to think about how the Trump tweets might be shaping their temporal experience. In the first instance, we might consider Trump-Twitter as a fraction of all-Twitter, so we can explore their experience of platform temporality. Subsequently, we might take that Twitter-centric experience and locate it relative to a wider event set – total screen time, for instance.

All inter-system interaction is a function of perspective – that is, the system's awareness of its place and its (inter)action in the wider systemic universe. In other words, a system has to attend to an event happening (through autopoiesis) in order for that event *to be meaningful* and, by extension, for it to produce time. Just as our own perspective limits our capacity to observe interaction between study systems, perspective also limits the meaningful interaction between the study systems. We can use this limiting function of perspective to describe the perspectival experience of a subject system. We simply say that a system's experience of its interaction within another system is determined by the amount of attention it pays to those interactions compared to the total amount of attention it pays to all interactions:

$$P_n = S_1 S_{2n} / S_{1n}$$

If we plug in some topical information from our Trump-COVID example, then we can expand this relationship to locate the temporal experience as I have just described it:

$$P_n = \left(S_1\ T_{Trump} / S_1 T_{All}\right) / S_{1n}$$

There are a couple of questions that we need to ask of this measure. First, I think we should query how valid it is to estimate perspective in this way. How reasonable is it to reduce that multi-variable phenomenon to a simple 'attention ratio'? Second, assuming that we decide it is valid, we should insist on more specificity. What does total system attention (S_{1n}) represent in the world?

Both questions ask us to consider what perspective means within the interaction field. In the Lorentz transforms, perspective is a positional construct – it presupposes a spacetime grid to position objects relative to each other, and uses coordinates defined by that grid to effect its transformations. However, recall that reality defined through assemblage and systems theory is event based – perspective is not defined by spatial coordinates, but by *event experience in the interaction field.* Ultimately, it does not matter *where* a system is within the field (even if that idea made sense) because that physical position would only be a proxy measure for the events actually experienced – that is, the events to which the system can attend. These are the events that produce time. For this reason, I would argue that it is absolutely valid to use an attention ratio to approximate perspective: no matter how complex the relations that shape perspective, the effect of those relations is to direct the system's attention towards some events and not others.

If we accept that the conceptualisation of the ratio measure is valid, we must next ask how feasible it is to implement. Can we realistically expect to measure different dimensions of system attention? Clearly, the challenge here is to interpret perspective in terms of events within the interaction field – and specifically in terms of events that are empirically available for study.

Located fully within the interaction field, it is easy enough to define what total system attention should be: it is the sum of interaction-events that the system attends to during the study period. However, included within that sum are presumably external-facing events (i.e. interactions between the system and its environment) but also internal-facing events (i.e. the events that make it possible for the system to attend to anything at all). It now becomes a little more difficult to interpret total system attention. In one count, we have the total number of interactions happening between the system and its environment; in another, we have the events simultaneously happening inside the system, but this count is a good deal harder to interpret. Presumably it includes events associated with the autopoietic response to the environment, as well as events associated with the system's 'inner life'. What does this mean? According to the systems-theoretic definition we are using, for any given system this inner life would constitute the subset of interactions between component sub-systems that register during autopoiesis.

This idea sounds very confusing, but it is easily grasped if we think of our common experience. Being biological systems, the human experience of the world is shaped in part by our internal biology – aches and pains, hormonal and chemical fluctuations, the rhythmical operations of our organs. Those organs are systems themselves, each a complex network of biological and chemical events maintaining function over time. Mostly, however, we do not register these events. Our kidneys filter our blood, our stomachs digest our food, and we do not attend to it happening unless something goes wrong and then a pain alerts us to the problem. Consider the multiple event-complexities necessary to keep our hearts beating (the electrical impulses firing, the valves opening and closing), yet we tend to notice only a single, linear pulse. Similarly, we may attend to the rhythm of our breathing, the lungs filling and emptying, but beneath that experience are millions of events dispersing oxygen from the lungs into the blood that we never sense happening. It is hard to imagine how those millions of 'hidden' events contribute to our experience of time. We assume that they contribute to the breathing rhythms that we can attend to directly – the breath entering and exiting our lungs, the rise and fall of the diaphragm and so on. These 'headline' events give shape to our internal temporal experience, they are the product of a communicative process that receives some signals loudly while barely registering others.

Autopoiesis is the process of event-response: it can be thought of as the liminal interface between the internal and the external worlds. Time is realised through this interface, so time is the interplay between internal and external event sequences. Therefore, if we want to ask what S_{n1} means 'in the world', the only possible answer is that it is the sum of the events attended to by a system, both internal and external:

$$S_{n1} = \sum (E_{int}, E_{ext})$$

In other words, S_{n1} is the total events in the subjective experience, and it therefore includes all the interactions with the specific system configuration that we are studying in our analysis of network time. S_{n1} does not represent the system's total hypothetical capacity to attend (much like the external world, the internal system is unknowably complex), but rather its total event-orientated *attention experience*. Consequently, we can rewrite the first of the perspective equations above:

$$P_n = \sum E_{ext} \Big/ \sum (E_{int}, E_{ext})$$

And the second:

$$P_n = \left(\sum E_{S_1 Trump} \Big/ \sum E_{S_1 Twitter} \right) \Big/ \sum (E_{int}, E_{ext})$$

This is the simplest 'form' of social time that we can model: it engages the subject S_1 directly in interaction with a subject system, $S_{Twitter.}$ Examples of this type of auto-empiricism might include a researcher interacting with their own social media feed, or a factory worker self-reporting the rhythms of the production line. In both cases, it is possible to argue that interaction is more complex than the simple framing suggests, but we can also devise ways to limit the temporal experience of that complexity. For instance, in the first example we could place the researcher in a low-stimulus room and limit their awareness of their social media to the push alerts that sound on their phone when an app updates. The record of their temporal experience therefore becomes their account of how their attention is distributed between their thoughts and the sound of their phone alarm.

Such cases are clearly limited, however, and assume that it is possible to control system interaction to effect this limitation. It would surely be better if we could establish a principle that could permit wider observation *as a function of perspective* and a method for synchronising these perspectives with one another. This would allow us to consider time-producing relationships between different systems, and perhaps even begin an assessment of influence between systems. We might ask quite complex questions connecting the temporality of our interaction with Trump-Twitter and the temporality of our political beliefs, our voting intentions or some other social domain or action – the writing of this book, for instance. More straightforwardly, we might attempt an observation of Twitter time from the perspective of a third party, moving beyond auto-ethnography, and perhaps eventually reach a method for combing multiple perspectives into a summary description of the phenomenon.

Really, this is the reason for engaging fully with perspectivism. It is important to recognise how perspective complexifies the subjective-seeming experience of time, but it is exciting to consider how its challenges may also point the way towards objectifying solutions. In theory, following Mead's (1938) assertion that reality is the sum of contributing perspectives, the task of combining perspectives should not be too taxing mathematically. There are two elements to the task. The sum of the interaction events from one perspective needs adding to the events from another perspective and the interactive relationship between the two perspectives needs quantifying.

The above equation, in which we engage an observing subject directly with the temporality of Trump-Twitter, defines the perspectival experience of that subject as it relates to a predefined set of time-producing interactions. In other words, provided that we clearly define a time-producing phenomenon in terms of the events that assemble it, then the equation is generalisable. We can use the same approach to estimate the perspectival experience of any system engaged with the interaction set. This is just another way of saying that there is nothing special about the status of the observer – ultimately, we are all subjective systems because we all have a limited perspective on the interaction field. The crucial thing to acknowledge here is that the estimation of perspective, P_n in the equation, is also an estimation of temporality. Time is the denominator of experience and so, for any given system *n* in the interaction field, $P_n = T_{Sn}$.

So how should we approach the challenge of combining perspectives? According to Mead (1938), universal objective reality is the sum of perspectives, but it is surely reductive to add one perspective to another and to assume that the total is time. The primary issue we face is that time is the relative differentiation between systems. If one system differentiates incredibly slowly and another very quickly, the time that they produce together is unlikely to be an addition of two speeds. Rather, the experience of time is captured in the *relative experience of the two speeds*, which is ratio measure.

Let's assume that we are focussed on a set of interactions between two systems, S_1 and S_2. We should differentiate between the two perspectives that the systems have on their shared experience, writing S_1S_2 when we want to denote the S_1 perspective and S_2S_1 to denote the S_2 perspective. We can describe the perspectives of the systems separately as follows:

$$S_{1n} = \sum E_{S_1S_2} / E_{S_1}$$

$$S_{2n} = \sum E_{S_2S_1} / E_{S_2}$$

Superficially, we might think that these two equations, arranged as they are above, appear similar to the physical equations that describe relative motion: the Lorentz transforms, which were mentioned earlier. I suppose that there are similarities, at least in the epistemological framework for approaching the problem – we approach relative differentiation via a positional description of the systems engaged in that differentiation, and only after that do we try to describe the changing relationship between these positions.

In theory, the outcome we seek, the T-RDIS model, is defined simply by the relative rates of differentiation captured by the summation of events in the two perspectival equations defined above. However, there is nothing else in these equations that concerns us. Time is simply a product of events and attention, and the relative distribution of those two things across two perspectives. Consequently, the time produced in the interaction between systems S_1 and S_2 is estimated by combining the two perspectival equations – there is no need for a transformation or a γ constant:

$$T_{S_1S_2} = \left(\sum E_{S_1S_2} / \sum E_{S_1}\right) / \left(\sum E_{S_2S_1} / \sum E_{S_2}\right)$$

This equation describes the temporal experience of the two spacemen floating in the otherwise empty universe. On one side of the ratio, spaceman S_1 observes his interactions with spaceman S_2 as a subset of all his interactions in the world (which, let's remember, are constructed through his internal monologue, because the universe is otherwise empty). On the other side of the ratio, spaceman S_2 makes observations of S_1 floating in the distance as a subset of his total awareness of the world (E_{S_2}). Under such circumstances, which I have argued are generalisable to a more complex interaction field, time is the distribution of attention between the different perspectives.

There is a problem, however: we are still lacking a crucial element, the absence of which renders the above equation basically meaningless. $T_{S_1S_2}$ is meant to the combined temporal experience of S_1 and S_2 but our equation doesn't give us any way of translating between those experiences. According to Nobert Elias (1993), time is the relationship between three continua of changes, two interacting systems and a third, which we need to standardise or regulate the interactive relationship. The $T_{S_1S_2}$ may be correct, but it doesn't give us any way to locate, to pin down, or otherwise make sense of the *always* changing relationship between S_1 and S_2. The fundamental difference between our simple time relationship equation and the Lorentz transform is that special relativity is predicated on complex physical laws that define possibilities for motion. We don't yet have anything that defines 'event possibilities'.

Synchronicity

Why do we not default to the physical laws that define spacetime and special relativity? The answer, simply – and at the risk of repeating myself – is that these physical laws do not adequately describe changes that may be social or symbolic, events that are textual or immaterial. If we are dealing with moments in the internal monologue of a floating spaceman, then it seems to me that these events are not adequately captured by a four-dimensional manifold that is predicated on motion. In one sense, our positional descriptions are far simpler: we are interested only in 'motion' in an abstract, figurative sense, as a familiar word for describing a change between states. We are not concerned with maintaining a physically viable orientation in spacetime, and we have nothing at all to say about universal constants or the speed of light. In other words, we are not operating within a defined physical spacetime grid.

Inevitably, though, the question of standardisation and the effort to regulate between perspectival systems demand some sort of 'independent' third system, and this automatically implicates the clock, because clocks perform this role universally in science and in much of society as well. When we write that science engages with time through the clock, what we really mean is that in science the clock always fulfils the role of the third continua of change. Scientists record measurements at specific 'times' that they describe using a clock, and that process of description is the same across most experiments. When social time theorists talk about clock time being 'hegemonic', they mean that the clock is fulfilling this same role by default outside the laboratory – in factories and in schools, in the media and in politics. But, having worked so hard to separate our understanding of time from our ideas about the clock, we must decide whether it is coherent, or helpful, or productive if we then invoke the clock to fulfil our standardisation needs. We see this problem time and again in writing about social time, even in books such as this one that are concerned primarily with the mechanics of phenomenon. I referenced the issue in Chapter 2, when I talked about how temporal language influences our understanding of time itself. Even once we have accepted the possibilities of pluritemporalism, we still rely on the clock to make sense of its variable complexities.

One way to think about the clock is to focus on our relationship with it. When we deploy a clock in our experiments we are really substituting ourselves for it, and saying that we do not trust our own temporality to pace our observations reliably or consistently. At the same time, we are pretending that by deploying the clock we have abstracted ourselves from the experiment: the clock is doing the temporal work so we don't have to. This isn't quite right, for the many reasons that we have already discussed. We remain implicated in the experiment because we have set it up: we establish the observing perspective, even when observations are mechanised, and we still have to interpret the relationship between the events recorded and whatever number the clock has appended to them. Often we don't think about this interpretative work, but it becomes obvious as soon as we have to think about the meaning of the timestamp in the wider study of network time. On Twitter, for instance, every tweet is given a Coordinated Universal Time (UTC) stamp when it is published, but the actual appearance of that tweet in the timelines of multiple Twitter users is distributed over a far longer, more variable and considerably more complex period. The 'origin time' of a tweet, therefore, is actually always variable, distributed somehow between the moment of publication and the moment of reception.

This interpretative work is an inescapable necessity in any sort of time study. Unfortunately, it further complicates Elias's (1993) temporal 'triangulation' idea, and most of what we have said about the production of social time. While time requires at least three change continua, in practice a fourth continua (the researcher or, more broadly, the human mind) is also required to interpret the relationship between the interacting and standardising systems. I think the easiest way to describe this relationship, and hopefully to make sense of it, is to use an illustration to show how events are distributed across continua.

Imagine two systems, S_1 and S_2, representing our two spacemen, each of which is aware of the other floating in an otherwise empty space. This 'awareness' is defined by acts of communication, the process of registering and interpreting an interaction within the system or between the system and its environment (i.e. the void and one spaceman floating in the distance). As far as our discussion is concerned, these communication acts *are events* – they are the happenings through which the world comes into being. For the moment, we will assume that all events are temporally equal because this will make it easier for us to visualise the difference between events that are simultaneous and those that are not. If we assume that all events have the same duration, regardless of the perspective in which they arise, then it is far easier to make assumptions about simultaneity and difference and these assumptions will simplify the work of synchronisation enormously. If we do not make this assumption, then the idea of the event becomes exponentially more complex. We will have to engage with questions of presentism and persistence and worry about the equivalence of perspectives, and the possibility that time dilates or transforms differently in the act of interpretation.

All that being the case, we can describe the interactions between our two spacemen using a simple sequence chart like the one in Figure 4.2. In the chart, each spacemen is represented by three event sequences. In line 1 are S_1's internal events; in line 2 are events that involve interactions between the spaceman and his environment – external events; in line 3 are a selection of those external events that involve interactions between the two spacemen $\left(E_{S_1 S_2}\right)$. The sum of these three lines is $\sum E_{S_1}$, the total event experience of the system.

Now, in our example, the second line, in which S_1 experiences a series of interactions involving the environment but not involving spaceman S_2, makes no sense because the environment is a void, or an event vacuum. The only interactions available to S_1 in that environment involve S_2 – otherwise S_1 is just reflecting on his internal monologue. It would be more accurate, then, to display line two as a series of dots without punctuating events or, more simply, to remove in entirely from our diagram, meaning that the event experience for S_1 can be drawn as shown in Figure 4.3.

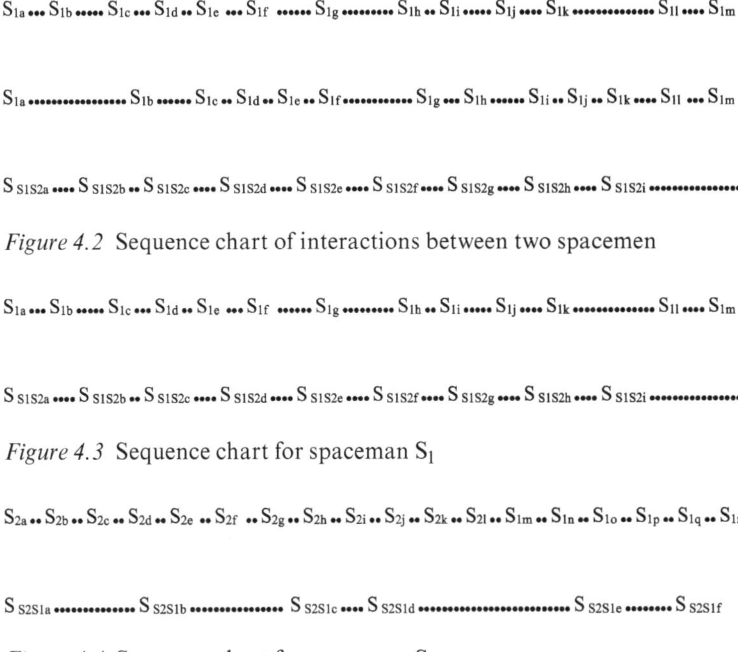

Figure 4.2 Sequence chart of interactions between two spacemen

Figure 4.3 Sequence chart for spaceman S_1

Figure 4.4 Sequence chart for spaceman S_2

We can redraw this diagram to represent the event experience of S_2, but let's assume that S_2 has a far more active internal monologue and spends far less time observing S_1 (Figure 4.4).

We can also combine these two diagrams to show how the respective event experiences align with each other. In Figure 4.5, the internal-external lines for the two systems mirror each other, so that interaction between the systems is represented in the middle of the diagram.

There are four highlighted interactions in the sequence shown in Figure 4.5, which represent cases where S_1 and S_2 are mutually aware of the interaction happening. They align in the sequence, which implies simultaneity, but their co-occurrence represents mutual recognition rather than anything fundamentally temporal (as yet, remember, there is no independent or external temporal 'structure' to give any sort of meaning to this idea). We might think of these highlighted events as follows: S_1 looks at S_2 and sees S_2 looking back at him – their eyes meet across the inky void. The other interactions, those that do not co-occur, might represent S_1 looking

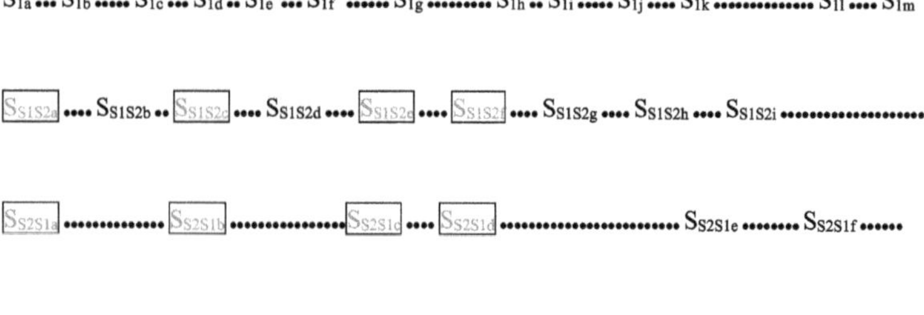

Figure 4.5 Sequence chart – synchronistic interaction between the systems

towards S_2 while he is rotating in space, facing another direction and unable to return S_1's gaze. In other words, it is possible for the two systems to interact and for that interaction to only register from one perspective.

What does that mean for the production of time? The truth is that it depends. We have assumed for this example that events are temporally equal, but we can see now that such an assumption is unlikely to hold for long. The temporal significance of an event depends upon the significance that a system assigns to it, which is, in turn, a product of how the system attends to the event. We might imagine that for each of our spacemen, those four moments when their eyes meet across the universe are elevated in some way above the unreciprocated interactions. We might recall a similar experience in a crowded room or at a party when we have caught another's eye and the moment has felt ripe with uncertainty and possibility. We focus our attention on such moments, mine them for hidden meaning – but in doing so, do we also affect time? Do we elevate those moments in our interaction with them, so that they set the rhythm of the period somehow? They do seem to step forward and demand our attention, ahead of all those other interactions that slip quietly by in the background, noticed but acknowledged less, as though their diminished significance also diminishes their power to push the world towards something new.

This, of course, is the real challenge of subjective time. Each of us – every perspective – is deeply implicated in time production because we direct our attention between interactions differently. So we might well assume that those mutually recognised interactions are interpreted differently by our two spacemen (a gaze returned is surely more significant when you are one of only two spacemen in the universe), but any difference arises through autopoietic interpretation. We can interpret the temporal influence of autopoiesis only if we have each spacemen explain its significance to us. We might then start to make adjustments to our sequences to emphasise the importance of synchronous interaction. Crucially, though, these temporal differences arise within the perspectives of our individual spacemen – a reciprocated glance might invoke *more* autopoietic activity, for instance, literally the production of more meaning. Otherwise, the interactions themselves, the events we are marking and trying to interpret, are ontologically equal.

Does this then mean that we can mark their happening against some sort of standardised and independent framework and be confident that we are marking happenings that are *quantitatively the same*? For some readers, this will remain a contentious claim – after all, it denies the elemental dissimilarity upon which the distinction between subjective and objective time is predicated. Bergson argued forcefully that events were not quantitatively the same and constructed his theories of different multiplicities upon this distinction. What have we actually done to address this argument?

Fundamentally, what the T-RDIS model does is separate the event from our interpretation of it. An event is just an event, and all events are equivalent. Hypothetically, even something like duration, which is often considered an elemental temporal phenomenon (e.g. Pöppel 1978), is not a trait of the event (which is given duration) but of the system giving duration to it (i.e. repetitive autopoietic processes that reinstantiate the happening of the event). In other words, events have no attributes. The differences that we recognise in events are the product of relative differentiation between systems, and specifically of perspectival autopoietic processes. The intuitive and emotional differences within a qualitative multiplicity are reflections of our own intuitive and emotional responses to events within the multiplicity set.

Using this logic, I think, we can justify the synchronisation of events using a standardised framework, but it leaves us facing two very challenging questions. First, we must decide whether there is something fundamentally temporal about our experience of events beyond the ratio of internal and external differentiation rates. That is, when social time theorists argue that phenomenological time speaks to something more profound and essential, are they telling us something fundamental about time that our T-RDIS model cannot capture? Second, if we decide that the logic holds, and standardisation and measurement are possible, what measure should we use? Specifically, given its pre-eminence in modern time discourse, we should decide whether the clock can fulfil this role.

What makes time?

Let's deal with the first question. Quite clearly, I have been trying to make the case that it is possible to conceptualise events beyond our human capacity to experience them, but I realise that there are possible objections to this case. According to the interactionist model, discontinuities between events arise from the autopoietic tendencies of the systems experiencing those events. Autopoiesis is a feature of all systems, so I would argue that everything has the capacity to experience time, including human beings obviously, but also other animals, things that we would normally think of as objects – like stones – and even things that we do not usually think of 'as being things': cultures, institutions and bureaucracies, for instance. I would also argue that phenomenological time, in focussing its attention on the human experience, has revealed much to us about that experience, but perhaps rather less about time itself. By locating time so fully within the *being* of humans, we have denuded it of its significance beyond us. In large part, T-RDIS is an effort to remake time as the denominator of all experience defined through the lens of perspectival interactionism.

In other words, the phenomenological study of time has revealed a great deal about our internal differentiation – that is, the autopoietic processes by which humans make meaning and time – but far less about the relationship between internal and external time production that we are seeking to describe here. T-RDIS doesn't preclude or deny the phenomenological study of time, but it does say that such work should be contextualised through its relations to the wider interaction field. As I have argued in previous chapters, social time study assumes that we are interested primarily in the study of humans-in-time and does not allow much room for thinking about time as a supra-human phenomenon. It also makes it virtually impossible to consider time contextually or to make comparisons between contexts and practices. Eventually, time ends up almost disappearing from the discussion altogether, so that descriptions of social time reduce to descriptions of social practices. It is a little like physics with the Block Universe: time is folded into other phenomena and forgotten.

So I am rejecting that idea. I think events have ontological status beyond the human capacity to experience them and, more contentiously, I am prepared to assume that events are ontologically equivalent. This raises another irritating metaphysical question, of course, because events only exist because of autopoiesis: events are interactions between systems, which means they cannot exist outside of autopoiesis. If a system does not recognise and respond to a happening *on some level*, than literally nothing has happened: the system persists unchanged. Surely, then, we cannot discuss events independently from the autopoietic perspectives that generate them?

This is tricky, but recall that we are using attention ratios as an approximation of autopoietic response. There is a certainly a discussion to be had around how valid it is to approximate complex phenomenology in this way – T-RDIS effectively reduces time experience to an attention ratio, and this may well overlook the more nuanced and intuitive dimensions of the experience. But the T-RDIS response to this challenge is that such experiences are peculiar to perspectives and to system complexity located at those perspectives – they are also 'supra' phenomenon; they are types of meanings that systems produce, so they are a result of producing time. In other words, we don't *need* nuanced and emotional humanity in order to have time. All we need is internal-facing attention and external-facing attention.

Without doubt, there is an elusive difficulty in this formulation, which is presumably why time has always proved such a confounding subject. It is relatively easy to say that time is defined by different continua of changes, but it is very hard indeed to locate those changes and explain their relationships to each other with any certainty. The T-RDIS model is meant to help with locating the change-events that matter in a time-producing relationship. It says that events happen when systems interact with each other, and it locates time in the respective autopoietic responses to those interaction events. As such, time is made on this liminal surface between internal and external awareness. Accordingly, the simplest possible time-production model involves two systems; a single system cannot, on its own, produce time. Let's think about this for a moment. A human being floating in empty space, aware of their own thoughts, is not producing time: to think is not sufficient. Time is only produced when there is something external to that human – a stimulus of some sort – to pace the rhythms of the internal reflective process.

Note that there is a sleight of hand in this example. It assumes that a human is nothing but their thoughts and not the product of biological complexity. Of course, a human is producing time because a human is an assemblage of constituent systems: organs interact, blood flows, cells respire. The interaction between these systems produces the time that then regulates their activity, but 'the human' (the Cartesian subject) is the bounding environment within which this time is made. For the human and their conscious mind, there is no internal-external surface on which to produce time for them – nothing that marks difference. In this strange hypothetical, the human is the universe, the sum of all interactions, time *t*, and still they have no sense of the concept.

In the examples to date, we have used a second spaceman to establish the time-producing relationship, but we could have used anything: a blinking light, a slowly rotating object or a clock counting its seconds and minutes. The point here is that there is nothing special about a clock: it is just another system, although admittedly it is one that we have engineered to differentiate itself with a regular, repeating action. This regularity allows it to fulfil the role specified by Elias – a third change continua to standardised or translate the relative changes within continua 1 and 2 (Elias 1993). We use the clock for this purpose for two very good reasons. The first is that we are accustomed to it – clock technology is universally accepted to the extent that most actors don't differentiate between the clock and the time that it is meant to translate for us. The second reason is that the clock is a very good standardisation system: modern clocks are highly engineered technologies, capable of differentiating with incredibly precise, consistent and reliable rhythms (Burdick 2017). This is why scientific engagement with time is so wedded to the clock: it is a highly sophisticated and highly socialised regulation tool.

So why do social time theorists, and especially pluritemporal time theorists, not use the clock to standardise the times they are trying to describe? In an earlier chapter, I suggested that scientific and social time theorists have never been further apart, and that the Einstein-Bergson debate largely settled matters in favour of the scientists. The clock played an important role in that settlement, not least because quantification is clearly preferred by the political and ideological projects of machine capitalism. The clock is identified with both science and capitalism, so for many social time theorists there a strong argument *not* to surrender social time to measurement, because doing so would concede all temporal domains to coercive capital power. The refusal to measure is an act of resistance.

However, this argument conflates a couple of dynamics that we might also consider separately. While it is true that measurement and clock time are generally considered *hegemonic together*, the systems-time definition treats them as separate phenomena. It does not concede that the clock measures time directly. The clock is just another system in the interaction field. It is a highly engineered system, of course – it differentiates according to a regular and quantifiable rhythm – and this means that it is a useful perspective from which to compare the relative times of subject and object systems. The clock is not time, though, nor does it measure time directly. It is simply a regulated system that we use to compare and synthesise the relative speeds of subject and object differentiation, as though it were the Newtonian constant. In this sense, reclaiming measurement from the clock seems like it might be liberating for social time – it could loosen capital's grip on the rhythms of our daily routines and re-energise the subjective experience of assemblage.

So what would our interaction model look like if we introduced a clock into the dynamic to work as a standardising system – an independent third continue of change? The answer is actually very simple and easily illustrated (see Figure 4.6).

The clock simply becomes a single additional row in the table. Inquiring minds may see a contradiction here. We have said that there is nothing special about the clock, that it is like any other system, just engineered to differentiate regularly and reliable. So how do we justify representing the clock as a single row

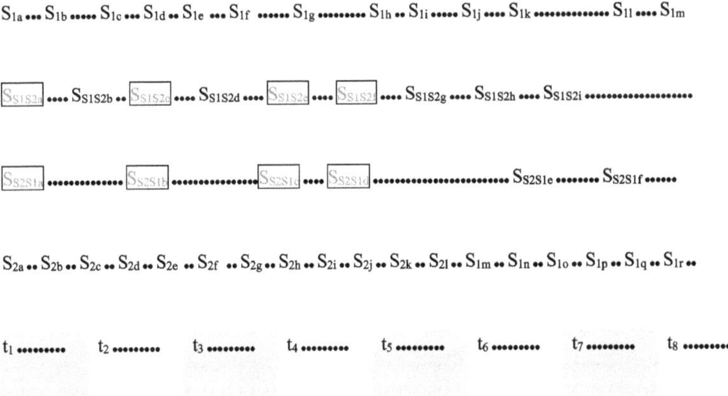

Figure 4.6 Sequence chart involving a clock

in the table? Surely it should be two rows like the other systems, an interactive entity capable of both external- and internal-facing differentiation?

This challenge is surely right, the clock should be two rows; it's artificial and reductive to display it as I have done. The clock doesn't measure time independently, it experiences time like any other system, and its actions are therefore implicated in the production of time. We *use* clocks in a way that ignores this complexity. There is a curious paradox in how we think about this practice. We like to think that clocks provide us with direct access to time – to the ticking of the universe – but, in fact, we use them as though they were 'extemporal'. We ignore their interactivity and abstract them from the world of time production, so that we can use them as time keepers. I think that this is the central contradiction that troubles our thinking about time. In order to make sense of time production, we invented clocks and imagined that they were somehow outside the process, and then we don't know quite how to reconcile this disjunction.

So how would it look if we tried to correct this artifice? Clearly the clock would be displayed as two rows, the one already displayed representing its internal differentiation and another that captures its experience of interaction in the world. It would look like any other system. The problem is that we find it almost impossible to imagine how this second row might look. What capacity does a clock have to attend to its becoming in the world? What events does it notice and what does it ignore? It is as hard to imagine the time experience of a clock as it to imagine the experience of a stone, or any other 'object' that we tend not to consider as interactive. The truth is that we are not particularly interested in the time experience of the clock – the rationale for engineering a technology with such a regular internal rhythm is that we want this internal rhythm to take precedence over any external-facing interaction. After all, that is the root of the clock's utility. The ticking of the seconds, minutes and hours is meant to dominate, to 'sound through' the temporal noise, and to impose regularity on the otherwise messy assemblage of interactive time. In effect, we pretend that the clock's internal rhythms 'override' its capacity for external time experience – we say: no matter what else happens in the world, the clock's time experience will always be shaped by the eternal ticking of its mechanisms.

The solution, therefore, is that we pretend that the clock is something that it is not: an extemporal and independent change continua, there to pace the relative action of other systems but not to become involved itself in the interaction field. Effectively, we treat the clock as Newton first proposed that we should, the only difference being that we do not call it 't' and we do not consider it time. Of course, this creates another issue, because if we are denying the clock any capacity to experience time for itself, then we also deny it any capacity to observe or record the events happening around it. For this to happen, then, we require systems that are independent of the clock and independent of the time production process, but capable of using the clock, like a lens, to bring into focus the interactive rhythms of their assemblage.

Observation

In theory, we can imagine our spacemen doing exactly this, each wearing a watch to translate their respective temporal experiences, and in practice we will be familiar with the experience, counting down the minutes left in a school lesson or the days until an anticipated date. When we do this, when we focus too much of our attention on the clock, we feel like we are losing touch with the experience of time being produced. We talk of time dragging, of seeming to slow, and we may feel like the clock works to separate us from time – that is, from the interactive frenzy of becoming. Alternatively, when we do find ourselves aware of time being made in a more irregular, chaotic fashion, we our confronted by the apparent asynchrony of the experience, the weird unmooring from the clock, and it can be stressful and disorientating.

This is what network time does. Modern digital media is programmed to be immersive for profit, algorithms are constantly gaming for our attention, and so it is unsurprising that we find ourselves becoming acutely aware of their temporal influence. The network detaches from the clock and immerses us in the rhythms of its own assemblage. The challenge, if we are going to find a way to describe and compare network times empirically, is to relate this temporal experience back to the clock's familiar and predictable rhythms – to somehow synchronise events between the interactive systems with internal ticking of the pretend non-interactive one.

In the case of the spacemen, it may be relatively easy to imagine this happening, because we focus on either spaceman and consider his or her experience directly. In the network, however, where we have multiple systems, both human and non-human, it is far harder to isolate and describe any one time experience, and far harder still to translate a collective experience back into clock time. Earlier in this chapter, we considered the case of an auto-ethnographic researcher carefully controlling her interactions with her smartphone to produce a simple example of network time experience. The graph above models this example. The researcher monitors her internal and external time experience; the smartphone differentiates itself and some of those happenings are observed by the researcher. A clock placed outside the room records all those happenings using its strict system for imposing temporal regulation. In effect, there are two interactive systems in this example and there is the clock, which we place outside the room to limit its interactive influence on the researcher.

While this scenario may work theoretically, we still face a problem. Who is responsible for doing the translation work, for documenting the experiences of the researcher and her smartphone and for interpreting these experiences using the abstracted clock? When I discussed this example previously, I suggested that the researcher do this work for herself, but in practice (and, indeed, if we are trying to limit the interactivity of the clock) we rarely want a single subject to self-report her network time experiences. More often than not, we are working with cases that involve several subjects – vast publics of social media users, for example – and we want to describe a collective sense of their temporal experience. Most of the empirical examples I discussed in Chapters 1 and 2 involve entire social media communities discoursing around a particular subject or topic. In such circumstances, the researcher is not necessarily located within the interactive experience; rather the researcher, like the clock, is pretending to be external to and independent from it.

So the synchronisation table in Figure 4.6 is still not capturing the complete picture. For most instance of network time, we want the time-producing interaction set, the clock for synchronisation and an observer (the researcher) to make sense of the various happenings (Figure 4.7).

We can also add the observing perspective to our event model, making clear that the instance of network time we claim to be observing is specific to the observing perspective O_1. In this equation, I have also included the t_n codifier to signify that we will be using a clock to synchronise events between sequences:

$$T_{S_1S_2|O_1} = t_n\left(\left(\sum E_{S_1S_2} \middle/ \sum E_{S_1}\right) \middle/ \left(\sum E_{S_1S_2} \middle/ \sum E_{S_2}\right)\right) \middle/ t_n \sum E_{O_1}$$

The equation now describes a complex relationship, so it may be worth articulating that relationship in plain English, to the extent

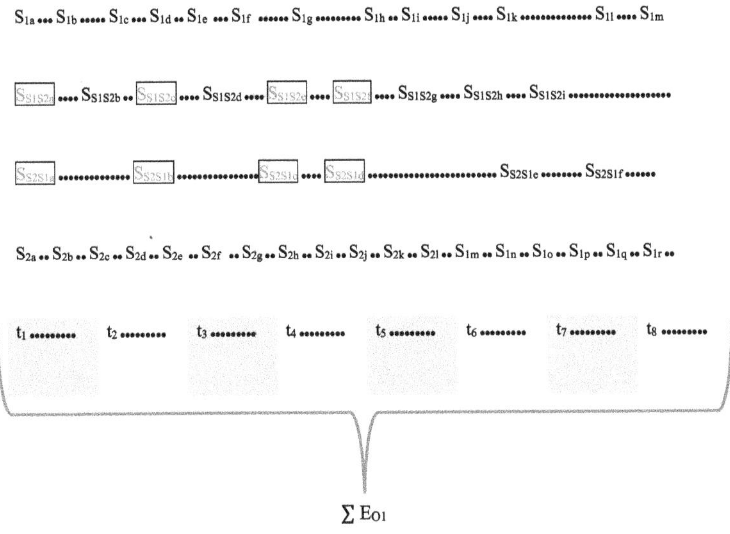

Figure 4.7 Sequence chart with clock and observer

that this is possible. Any instance of social time (T) is defined by the interacting systems that produce it (S_1S_2) and the observing perspective that describes it (O_1). In the above example, there are two systems (S_1 and S_2) that produce time when they interact with each other. For each system, the time produced through interaction is a subset of the time produced by every event that the system experiences in the corresponding period. In other words, for each system time is a calculation in which the nominator is instance-specific events and the denominator is all events. The time produced between two interacting systems is a ratio in which time production in one system is aligned with time production in the other system. The description of this time is made by an observer (O_1), for whom the time observations are the nominator in its own time production calculation in which total event experience $\left(\sum E_{O_1}\right)$ is the denominator. All these events across all these perspectives are synchronised using a clock measure (t_n), which for the purpose of the description we assume is independent from the subject systems.

These are the relationships that we must describe if we want to make network time available for empirical study. We require a full accounting of the events producing time between the interacting systems and we require a reasonable estimation (if an exact measure is not possible) of the underlying event-activity of each of those systems. Simultaneously, we require a fully articulated position from which to observe these events happening and we require a clock that operates across the entirety of the system, which we can then use to sequence and synchronise the different event-sets. In Chapter 5, I conclude my discussion of network time with an analysis of what these different variables might look like for common network time experiences.

References

Bergson, H. (1999 [1922]) *Duration and Simultaneity.* Manchester: Clinamen Press.

Burdick, A. (2017) *Why Time Flies: A Mostly Scientific Investigation.* New York: Simon & Schuster.

Elias, N. (1993) *Time: An Essay.* Oxford: Blackwell.

Hall, S. (1996) The question of cultural identity. In S. Hall, D. Held, D. Hubert and K. Thompson (eds), *Modernity: An Introduction to Modern Societies.* Oxford: Wiley-Blackwell, pp. 596–632.

Lewis, J. (2008) *Cultural Studies: The Basics.* London: Sage.

Mead, G.H. (1938) *The Philosophy of the Act*, ed. C.W. Morris et al. Chicago, IL: University of Chicago.

Pond, P. (2016) *Software and the struggle to signify: Theories, tools and techniques for reading Twitter-enabled communication during the 2011 UK riots.* Doctoral dissertation, RMIT University. Available at: https://pdfs.semanticscholar.org/4f11/cf76b5f86a6a04532e88b2b83b9776881dd6.pdf?_ga=2.85451993.1502538894.1609397109-305174746.1609307170. Accessed 29 December 2020.

Pöppel, E. (1978) Time perception. In R. Held, H.W. Leibowitz and H.-L. Teuber (eds), *Perception.* Berlin, Heidelberg: Springer Berlin Heidelberg, pp. 713–29.

Tada, M. (2018) Time as sociology's basic concept: A perspective from Alfred Schutz's phenomenological sociology and Niklas Luhmann's social systems theory. *Time & Society*, 28, pp. 995–1012.

5 Measuring network time

Introduction

The final chapter of this book provides a brief and focussed discussion of what an instance of network time should look like using the T-RDIS model as defined in the preceding chapters. It aims not to remake the argument for network time measurement, but to articulate what that sort of measurement involves when it is attempted in the world, and it will include a discussion of the various assumptions and trade-offs that are required. There are two main parts to this discussion. First, I will consider what sort of events need to be counted when we are attempting network time measurement. In short, I aim to move the methodological discussion beyond its current state under the practice of digital time-series analysis. That will involve a discussion of the relevant interacting systems and the relationship between interaction events and the systems' productive capacity. Second, I will discuss the different criteria that can shape an 'observation perspective', particularly the role played by digital methods in the process. It is crucial that we realise just how much influence our *capacity to access* the digital system has on the phenomenon we eventually observe. The discussion in this concluding chapter will largely avoid data and calculations. The aim here is not to demonstrate the mathematics of social time measurement but rather to ground that practice in a discussion of applied theory.

I have written elsewhere about the empirical challenge of locating events within specific digital systems, such as the micro-blogging platform Twitter (Pond 2020b), so I want to provide a more general account of what constitutes 'events' in digital networks. This is a necessary and important task: as we have discussed, network time is the product of network events. There can be no account of network time, no attempt to synchronise the production of meaning across multiple perspectives, without first a detailed cataloguing of the 'things that happen' within the network to produce meaning. However, if we focus on only one platform – or indeed a specific community or function located within that platform – while we may demonstrate the feasibility of the model, we will miss some of the general features of event-orientated network time. Of course, network time is produced locally, but it must also be produced in a more general sense across the entire network. Somehow, we must be able to identify shared temporal characteristics within the network that can differentiate network time from other instances of social time, otherwise the term itself makes no sense. We have asserted that network time is qualitatively different – faster, fluid, asynchronous – but what is it exactly that makes it so?

Locating events within the network

I have described a theory of events in this book, but it has been an abstract exercise. According to the systems differentiation model, events are communication acts that happen in the liminal space within and between systems. They are the *action* of autopoiesis. This can be a hard idea to visualise. There is something pleasing and poetic in locating time in the making of meaning, the process of assembling of the world, but it is a difficult formulation that is not materially obvious. If network time is made by network events, what are those events? Where are they located and what systems do they implicate?

An analysis of network time must therefore begin with a search for the systems that interact and constitute the 'network'. More precisely, we should say we are seeking systems that interact to produce meaning at the 'level' of the network. This phrasing is important because it emphasises a crucial feature of the interaction field. Wherever we are located within it, whatever the scale of our inquiries, there will be systems 'below' us, interacting to produce the phenomenon that interests us, and there will be systems 'above' us, creating a macro-phenomenon of which we are all components (Pond 2020a). In other words, system complexity *is scalar*: all systems are built from component systems and all systems are themselves components of more complex systems. That means that if we want to define and locate a time-producing system for study, then we can take two possible approaches. We can either begin with the macro-system that interests us and work recursively to define and locate events within its autopoiesis, or we can start with the component parts – the sub-systems that we think are fundamental to the assemblage – and try to observe interactions between them.

How should we approach the network time system, then, given that we know in advance that we will eventually be searching for events that contribute to the production of meaning at multiple system levels? Another way of asking this question is to query how meaning is made. A full discussion of this problem is largely beyond the scope of this book, but it is important to acknowledge that the proposed systems model assumes that meaning is produced locally first (though interactively with the environment), and then aggregated (and reproduced) across the network. This idea is articulated most clearly, perhaps, in the concept of externalism or networked knowledge – concepts that emphasise the collectivised and culturally embedded production of knowledge (Hartley and Potts 2014; Lewis 2008). It is an idea upon which I have leant heavily in my articulation of the *digital system*, which I consider the production of interaction between three discrete sub-systems: code, human users and hypertext.

The end point of this argument is that meaning is not located within individual users of the internet but rather distributed across it, floating in 'probabilistic clouds between systems, only becoming fixed when a specific system takes a specific perspective on the cloud (an event), thus assigning attention for a particular time to a particular array of sign-signified relations' (Pond 2020a: 197). This idea leads us towards a study of meaning through discourse, which we can imagine pulsing through the channels and tubes of the networked media. The likelihood of an individual interacting with a specific discourse – that is, a specific configuration of meanings encoded through hypertextual signifiers – is largely dependent on the 'volume' of traffic both within and across different channels. It is a remarkably crude or 'blunt-force' signification environment (Lewis and Best 2003), in which the loudest voices and most relentless messaging tend to dominate. A concept that usefully captures the experience of social media meaning-making is 'ambience', or the sense of being surrounded by and subjected to a dominating discourse or set of signifiers (boyd 2011). The notion that there are ambient discourses headlining the production of meaning on social media creates a useful benchmark for comparing influence and for grounding a search for user–code–text interactions that help produce or shape different emphases within that discourse (Pond and Lewis 2019).

Obviously, this is not the only way to define the internet or to approach it for study, and this raises questions for the study of network time, which is clearly influenced by these initial assumptions around how the internet produces meaning. In effect, my initial conceptualisation of the internet as a meaning-producing machine will inevitably influence where I go looking for the events I deem part of this process. This means that the network times I eventually measure are the outcome of my initial framing – in effect, they exist in the subjective interpretation of the researcher. This, however, is completely expected. Measures of network time will always require contextualisation because the network is only ever experienced locally. The researcher is always implicated in the framing of this local experience (and we will consider some important ways in which the researcher can influence his experience of the network later in this chapter). The key requirement is that we are clear in this contextualisation – that is, we must locate our analyses of network time in a clear statement of what we think the network is and how we think it is assembled.

So it is important to state that I consider the internet to be a techno-social assemblage, an interaction between discrete systems in the technological (code), social (people) and cultural (hypertext) domains. This doesn't mean that these are the only systems implicated in the network, but it recognises the influence of these systems, and it elevates the significance of their influence in terms of meaningful action. This statement about what I think the internet is also directs me in my search for events. Provided I can articulate the 'meaning' that the internet produces, I can ask: What are the interactions between code, people and text that affect this meaning-making process?

As stated, we are looking for interactions that produce some sort of change in the 'headline' discourses – those that are ambient within the network we are studying. As discussed in Chapter 2, that search has largely led researchers to focus on the publication of content that appears to contribute to these discourses. Weltevrede et al. (2014) pace the publication of *new* text relating to a major news event: widespread flooding in Pakistan in 2010. This leads them to capture new tweets, Facebook posts, Google news articles and other content that includes relevant key words and then use the publication timestamps to locate these interactions temporally. Thelwall (2014) proposes a similar method for Twitter specifically, using hashtags or keywords to define issues of ambience and then using each moment of publication to organise time-series analyses. This is what I did also in my doctoral work, comparing trends, topics and hashtags temporally using the volume of tweets published at five-minute intervals.

As we have established, there are issues with representing time through a single perspective without any sense of interaction happening or acknowledgment of perspective. There are also issues with conflating the publication of content with the production of meaning through that content. In any social media network, the instance of publication is always only the first temporal marker in a much longer, more complex and more diffuse meaning-making pathway. The moment of publication marks a single interaction between a single user and a hypertext configuration that may or may not expand, change and be reimagined as soon as it finds reception. This is both an important conceptual point about the instability of meaning and the deconstructive influence of the decoder (Hall 1980) and a practical point about the obvious dynamics and experience of social media communication. The posting of new content rarely marks the end of the meaning-making process – in fact, normally we are far more interested in what happens to content once it has been published and entered circulation than we are in the moment of its origin.

If we want to capture the temporality of discourse on networked media, and for it to be meaningful, we will need to record a far wider range of event types, including publication events, as part of an expansive set of interaction indices. Some of these indices will be platform specific. On Twitter, for instance, the retweet indicates an interaction between a human user and text, which is then encoded into a computational object that has a specific meaning with the Twitter machine and user culture. Other interactions are more comparable across platforms. A response or a reply to a tweet is functionally very similar to a comment on a Facebook post, although of course there are different emphases in the affordances of these interactions. Eventually, network time measures will need to engage with these affordances and the weight of influence they engender, but to begin with we are assigning all interactions the same status, so the task is easier: we *just* need to identify all the interactions.

There are two phases to this work. As described in the previous chapter, the eventual aim is to differentiate between events that are context and perspective specific and those that are denominating system activity. We must collect the latter of those data types before we can differentiate the former. In other words, we need the sum of the activity in the system-set we are investigating before we can untangle the various perspectives implicated in it. Unfortunately, there is no easy or predefined method here, and there will always be events that we miss. Recall that the total number of event possibilities is infinite because internal system activity is a chaotically complex and universal system activity – as we regress through constituent systems, through smaller and smaller scales of inquiry, the number of potentially relevant systems grows exponentially. Think of the human body, which in macro terms we define as a single perspective, but which contains billions of cells interacting with one another.

Given this complexity, our aim should be to identify the events that are most meaningful to the production of network time in the specific context that we have defined for study. This happens to be a very helpful formulation because it allows us to prioritise certain types of event, accepting that there others happening in the background but leaving them there because they are unlikely to exert much influence over the system *at the scale we are studying* it. This seems a perfectly valid assumption to make because multiple studies have demonstrated the uneven influence of different types of event on the production of discourse (e.g. Pond and Lewis 2019). In the vast majority of social media systems, for instance, user accounts that have large followings exert enormous influence over audience attention and, by extension, the distribution of ambient discourses. So it should be possible to propose a list of candidate events based on our existing knowledge of the different platforms, practices and users that we know are implicated in discursive activities. Table 5.1 presents some examples of this work, defining an event for capture, with a short explanation of how that event type is situated within the systemic production of meaning. In all cases, the event represents *action in the system* and influence is derived from the context of that action.

The empirical analysis of network time must begin with a period of focussed data capture, deploying a range of methods to record as many of these event types as possible. The selection of those methods is largely a function of necessity – in the social media sphere, Facebook's restriction of access to its application programming interface (API) following multiple scandals is also restricting research into the company's multiple entities and websites. Access to data from news and commerce websites is equally hard to obtain. However, the decision should not be based solely on practical concerns. The choices we make about how we design our methods have consequences for the data we eventually capture. We do not have total system access and the perspective we construct through our methodological approach is implicated in the network time we observe. In the next section, I discuss what some of these implications

Table 5.1 A selection of different event types on different platforms with short explanation

Event type	*Description*	*Examples*	*Notes*
Encoding event	An interaction between a human and hypertext, an encoding event produces meaning (through signification) at the system level for interpretation by multiple sub-systems. Encoding events generate media: texts, images, videos and other system-specific signifiers.	Content post (e.g. YouTube upload, Facebook post, tweet)	It may be possible in the future to conceive interactions between machines and text that can be classed as 'encoding' events, but machine–text interactions are currently classified 'logical operations' in this schema.
Decoding event	A decoding event represents another human–text interaction, in which a human user downloads media from the system and interprets it self-reflectively (i.e. through its own autopoietic processes).	A response to content comment (Facebook, Instagram, YouTube), reply, retweet or quote tweet (Twitter), reaction or vote (Instagram)	Decoding events are rarely available for direct observation, but instead must be inferred by an encoding event that is logically the product of decoding and reaction.
Network event	A transmission event involves a human–human interaction made via the technological system.	New user connection (e.g. new following relationship, Twitter, Instagram, Facebook friendship, etc.)	A network event represents a reconfiguration of a particular type of user network, in which connections are established through structural code rather than through communicative actions.

(*Continued*)

Event type	*Description*	*Examples*	*Notes*
Deferred event	A deferred event is one that's potential is empirically observable but its happening is not. In other words, a deferred event is one that exists only probabilistically: it can be inferred but it cannot be confirmed owing to limiting system access.	Hyperlinks, media, polls or other calls to action embedded in post or reply.	A deferred event is an action that is implied in the system but cannot be confirmed via the perspectives through which the system is normally accessed. As such, both the happening and the timing of the happening are uncertain. There are ways to confirm the happening, of course – direct user interviews, perhaps – but normally the event must be treated as uncertain during any synchronisation effort.
Logical operation	A logical operation involves a pre-programmed interaction between a machine and text or a machine and the human population, normally results in a reconfiguration of signifiers and, sometimes, the production of new signifiers according to coded instruction.	Update to trending topics (Twitter); news feed generation (Facebook); recommended post or video lists (e.g. Reddit or YouTube)	Encoding events involve a reconfiguration of relations within data structures, or between data and the encoded instructions that operate on that data. These events are 'substratum' for most perspectives

are and ask whether they can be resolved so our methods can be usefully standardised.

Methods and the observer perspective

The list of events in Table 5.1 makes a couple of things clear. First, in all but the smallest and most simple systems, there are multiple event types that configure different interacting systems into an assemblage that has an empirical duration. For some types of event, that duration seems very short, but for others it is clearly longer and represents a more 'complex' type of interaction. What we realise is that the events we can observe are representations only of more complex interactive behaviours, making them a knot of tangled temporalities, which somehow we should try to interpret. A retweet, for instance, is recorded as a single event with a specific timestamp, which marks the moment the user hit the retweet button to pass an original tweet on to their followers. However, this action-moment only happens after the user has received, decoded and interpreted the original tweet and decided that its message is worth forwarding. So, from the user's perspective, there are multiple interactions with the system that precede the moment of the retweet but are largely hidden from us as observers.

The dynamics are more complicated still because not all retweets are decided in the same way following the same interpretative dynamics. Not only do different users vary in their retweeting practices, not all users are even really users at all. Estimates vary wildly, but somewhere between 10 and 60 per cent of accounts on Twitter may be automated actors (bots), depending on the context, with political discourses being particularly susceptible to bot activity (Alothali et al. 2018; Chen et al. 2017; Wojcik et al. 2018). So, while we should not look to exclude bots from our analysis because they clearly contribute to the event-dynamics that shape systemic action, we should also recognise that they further complicate the idea that an event is a singular and uniform happening within the system.

The reason for this, if it is not already clear, is that every event is an assemblage of different interacting systems. It matters what those systems are and how they are situated in relation to the interaction, partly in terms of their position and their perspective, but also in terms of the autopoietic history through which they have arrived in that moment. I am not suggesting that we should try to capture and interpret all those subjective histories, because even if we could, how would we then align them with each other? Translating between the machine's 'language' of reproduction, encoded in loops, logical operations and conditional statements, and the messy, cultural human user is probably impossible and not really necessary for temporal analysis. This is unnecessary because we have already said that network time is all defined from the perspective of an observer, who most likely cannot access and is not interested in the diverse interpretative histories of the systems being observed. If we can return to our floating spacemen very briefly, we can see that the temporal experience of the first spaceman is shaped by what the second spaceman is doing in relation to his own internal activity – the equivalent experience of the second spaceman does not matter to him because he has no access to it. In the T-RDIS model, autopoietic actions matter only when they are empirically available for interaction with other systems.

However, this means that the autopoietic history of the observer *is* very much relevant to the observation and interpretation of network time. In the model proposed in the previous chapter, the observer is represented by a single positional statement, $t_n\left(\sum E_{O1}\right)$, which functions as the denominator for the entire model. While this statement works as a mathematical representation of the observer's significance, it hardly captures the variable complexities necessary for the observer to arrive at the moment of observation. In other words, $t_n\left(\sum E_{O1}\right)$ represents a complex network of observation assumptions – about where, when and how to look – capabilities and affordances, technicities and epistemic practices. We need to think about some of those things before we can begin capturing data from digital networks because those assumptions will shape the methods we use and the observations we eventually make.

Earlier in this chapter, I wrote that the methods we deploy to capture event data will influence what we observe via those methods. If we access a network system through a series of API queries, it will look different from how it presents through web scraping, participant observation or any other type of digital method. In one sense, this is quite an obvious assertion – an API query returns a gamut of metadata that is not available to the web scraper, which thus encodes API events with interactive potential that never pass through from the back end into hypertext mark-up language (HTML). Even within a single method, however, the observer is implicated in the 'vision' of the system that emerges – for instance,

> although the API can give an impression of 'total system access', and is often interpreted this way in research, this is not the case. The API is still only a single perspective on a system. It reveals some events but obscures others. The API perspective is limited in several ways but perhaps most significantly we limit it ourselves when we structure our queries to target certain data records.
>
> (Pond 2020b: 10)

The important point about API access is that it is internally variable. It is always the case that the data the platform records about itself and its users are the product of decisions encoded in software, taken by engineers, that prioritise certain types of events and deprioritise others. Moreover, the vast majority of APIs, and certainly those maintained by the dominant social media companies, restrict access to their data in crucial ways. Twitter famously maintains different streaming tiers, with public access limited to approximately 5 per cent of the total data produced by the platform. Facebook has now effectively shut down API access, but even before it did, enormous troves of data were privatised or available only to advertisers or third parties prepared to pay. These restrictions shape querying practices. Even if one assumes that there are no systematic biases affecting the public samples, the threat of rate limiting means a researcher must decide in advance a sampling approach that best suits their purpose. Often this translates into keyword-driven research, in which the total number of tweets requested is decided by a request for a particular set of keywords or topics, or a network-driven approach, in which data is requested for named accounts and their associates. Importantly, these two approaches construct different views of the digital system, and emphasise very different meaning-making dynamics. They also produce different data sets and thus different representations of network time.

Some researchers might suggest that a solution is to open and maintain an unfiltered query, requesting all the availability data from the system, then working on that data locally to explore the relationship between semantics and human relations. In broad terms, I support this approach – especially for network time calculations – but I have a couple of points to note in response. First, this assumes that the researcher has the capacity to store datasets that are much larger that they would otherwise be, and to operate upon them, which is not always the case. Second, this sort of data collection really depends on API access, so is not available for many of the instances of network time we might want to study.

An important thing to recognise about these two different types of query is that they emphasise different sub-systems within the network. If we query an API for keywords or for hashtags, or if we use a more complex method and query a range of topics or textual indicators, we prioritise the influence of text within the meaning-making system. If we send a query that lists a number of user accounts, and then asks for followers or friends, then we are prioritising the human–human relations that we imagine the network represents somewhere in the world. Neither of these approaches is obviously wrong, and nor is one clearly better than the other – the point is that the method we chose is most likely a reflection of *our own interpretative lens* and the conceptual framework through which we are imagining the system.

In other words, our own autopoietic action shapes how we approach the system of study, most often through the methods we deploy to enable that study. The 'scientific' response to this problem is clear: we should aim to standardise our methods and we should aim to control those factors that we cannot standardise through our experimental design. The problem is that standardisation is difficult because, as we have already discussed, different networks require that we use different methods to access data from them. While it is still possible to access data from Twitter via its API, and while YouTube offers a different but still relatively accessible API, Facebook and Instagram do not support API access – data must be collected through web scraping or opportunistic 'workarounds'.

So what can we do? We recognise that the observer is implicated in the measurement of network time in at least two different ways: they frame a system for study through autopoiesis and they interact with the system during observation, a dynamic that is shaped both by their observational capacity and by the system's own 'willingness' to be observed. As I have said repeatedly throughout this book, an observer represents just another perspective – where the observer is located and its capacity to observe together shape the reality it sees assembling around it. Technical discussions about API access, web scraping techniques and database structuring are all reflections of this simple statement concerning localisation within the interaction field.

There are three alternatives, I think, for how we chose to respond. The first of these draws directly on the argument from Percy Bridgman (1949) that observation itself elevates the reality of one perspective above all others: for Bridgman (1949: 354), it is 'obvious' that quantification – specifically, the ability to quantify – imbues experience with certainty, meaning that we prioritise the reality we can record above all the possible realities that we cannot. For our purposes, we could claim that our current ability to measure (which, let's not forget, is dependent upon methods that are themselves mediating technologies) underwrites the reality of the network times we end up recording. This response would at least address the first of our perspectival concerns. Rather than worrying about the interactions we might be missing, or the alternate dimensions of network time assembling through different perspectives, we prioritise the data that we can record and locate network time fully within its descriptive capacities. We would still, of course, face the challenge of standardisation – of finding a set of methods that we could deploy in the same fashion regardless of context – but, provided we were seeking multiple event types, as I described in the first part of this chapter, then I think we could credibly claim we had advanced network time empiricism a little bit.

The issue is that the Bridgman formulation sidesteps the reality of perspectivism, which is something I have spent considerable time arguing for in this book, so perhaps unsurprisingly I am not wholly satisfied with this solution to our problem. Yes, it simplifies the recording of network time, essentially imposing an assumption of scientific realism on the phenomenon, but that actually denies a great deal of what *feels real* about network time. Notably, it does not present as uniform – it does not feel as if one network time is elevated above all others. To my mind, it presents as multiple, discursive realities, which a user slips between while navigating their way through the hyperlinked web. One of the key points about network time is that one can move between its variable temporalities without realising it: a user can click on a link in a Facebook post and be sucked into a YouTube feed while WhatsApp notifications ping relentlessly in the background. 'What emerges is a "timeless time" or a "non-time" without past and without duration' (Weltevrede et al. 2014: 129).

Attention switching is key in this dynamic. The observer maintains the capacity to redirect their attention at any time so, even if we augment our prioritisation of a single perspective with a complete positional account, fully caveated, describing all the decisions and the assumptions that have produced it, we are still faced with a problem: these things can change. Our observations cannot happen outside of time – in fact, they are bound to change and when they do our perspective on the system we are studying is likely to shift a little.

So perhaps we should pursue a very different approach and try to multiply our observations to the greatest possible extent and capture as many perspectives on the system as we can. Theoretically, if we wanted to capture time-bound assemblage within the system *as a whole*, we would have to occupy all the possible perspectives within the system: every machine, every human user, every competing discourse. This isn't possible, of course, neither practically nor conceptually. Even the simplest networked system is a multivariable complexity that fragments into impossibly numerous perspectives at the slightest provocation. Perhaps, though, we could take a sample of this unwinding multiplicity, recognise the perspectives of both the machines and the men, and try to embed our observations more fully in the shifting rhythms of this multi-stranded timescape.

We will have to decide somehow which perspectives we should recognise and which ones we are happy to ignore. We will never fully capture the experience of these perspectives because our access to them will always be limited, so we will also have to deal with the fact that our observations are probabilistic. However, we can make progress at least, as long as we can decide upon some objective criteria to differentiate between those perspectives that are directly implicated in the production of network time and those that are not. Somehow, we must aim for a 'description of a limited but representative sample of perspectives, and then try to fold those perspectival accounts into a single empirical description of network time' (Pond 2020b: 11).

What should be the process for selecting these differentiating criteria? Given what we know about the interactive assemblage of systems, and given what we have discussed about autopoiesis, I think we can argue that the perspectives we need to include are those that exert *significant influence on ambience in the study system*. In other words, to deliver a comprehensive empirical account of network time, we must be able to *identify and locate* those interactions that shape meaning-making in the networked system we are studying. How should we identify influence? Influence is decided through autopoiesis. Influential interactions are those that prompt a greater autopoietic response from the system-set – literally, influence can be 'counted'. A post on Facebook that prompts 100 comments from different users is more influential than one that prompts ten comments – it is that simple. All we need to do is decide an influence threshold and then track the systemic action that pushes an autopoietic response above this threshold:

> When an event happens, the system can only respond through further events – that, after all, is a fundamental principle of event-based assemblage. An interacting sub-system (a perspective) can exert influence on systemic assemblage as long as its interaction with the system precipitates further events. The more event-responses that it can initiate, the greater its potential to

> influence the production of meaning within the system. Influence is therefore realised and measured through causal chains of interaction-events.
>
> (Pond 2020a: 232)

We can use this idea of influence to identify the different perspectives within the network – each of which will represent a system of code, human action or text – for which we need to record event sequences. It will depend on the network how many different perspectives are required, but as a rule of thumb we can use experience and reasonable estimation to set an initial number. For instance, typically most publics online are dominated by a few users who are responsible for most of the content and most of the interaction – often the distribution of user activity follows a power-law curve.

Finally, methods

So we have a way of deciding on a selection of perspectives implicated in the production of ambient meaning in the networked system we are attempting to study. We have a list of the different types of events that each of those perspectives may be experiencing, and a mathematical framework for synchronising those events through the T-RDIS model. In theory, then, we should be ready to plan for the recording of specific instances of network time. I want to finish this book by doing exactly that – by spelling out a series of steps to start recording network time using recognisable and accessible digital research methods.

1 Time production is system bound, so the first step in any measurement effort is to define the system of study. For network time, we will have to decide where we want to make our observations within the network. Are we interested in a specific platform or a discourse community located on that platform? Perhaps our interests are even more localised – we may want to investigate a small friendship network and track its interactions across Facebook, Instagram and Twitter. We may simply want to explore the temporality of our own media consumption. This first step is foundational in every sense. It is necessary to start a study, but it is also theoretically essential to frame the research, to identify the interacting systems of interest and to initiate the process of event-data collection.

2 Data capture begins as an exploratory process – an attempt to discover as many interactions as possible within the study frame. The methods deployed will depend on the platforms and technologies implicated by the framing work – Facebook and Instagram, for instance, are only partially available and require web scraping; data collection can still be automated for Twitter and YouTube. The aim of this exploratory work is to identify as many interacting systems as possible – user accounts, algorithmic logics, recurrent signifiers and so on. Once these systems have been identified and classified, their influence can be assessed. This is a quantitative process. Events that precipitate more events have influence – the greater the multiplicative effect, the greater the influence.

3 The second step delivers a list of systems that appear influential in the assemblage of the study frame (step 1). The third step involves a concentrated effort to locate the interactivity of those systems in the study period. Again, a mixed digital methods approach will be necessary to capture events located within different publics, different software structures and different discourses. This is intensive work, and it is likely to limit the measurement of network time to relatively short periods. Interactivity increases exponentially as the list of candidate systems grows longer, so a high level of automation will be necessary. Data are captured for each perspective, meaning that all interactivity is relevant. For instance, if our focus is the temporality of a friendship network, then we require all the interactions of the members of that network. That includes interactions with the friendship group, obviously, but also interactions with other accounts, other content and other code. Depending on how we have chosen to frame our study, we may even require a full account of each user's digital activity, including other platforms, services and media types.

4 The final phase in the methodology involves the integration of the event data into the T-RDIS model. It will probably involve several steps to ensure that data are processed, timestamped and properly formulated for synchronisation. Frame-specific data will need to be aligned and compared with (our estimate of) total system activity. Fairly high-powered computation will be required to do this simultaneously across multiple perspectives. The result will be a measure – an attention ratio – that we can track over a time-series, using intervals appropriate to our study frame.

This ratio will mean little to readers without contextualisation and some sort of comparative frame to make it sensible. The implicit logic of pluritemporalism is that one instance of social time only makes sense relative to another. Visual methods can help to illustrate the rhythmic fluctuations of the network, reflecting surges of interactivity, allowing researchers to pull at the different perspectival strands and to see how some systems exert more influence over the temporal frame than others. Beneath these visualisations, granular data locating different systemic interactions will still be available for those interested in deconstructing the mechanics of network time production.

At least, that is the aim. The project to make network time measurable remains in its infancy. At present, the theoretical arguments outlined in this book still need to be proved, and there are likely to be many objections from members of the social time fraternity. My hope is that those objections will engage with the substance of the arguments presented and with the possibilities towards which they point. As I said early on, my treatment of both scientific and social time theory is necessarily limited in a book this length. I wanted to establish the potential for temporal reconciliation and fully accept that there is more work to do – both conceptual and practical – to demonstrate this potential and prove its validity.

References

Alothali, E., Zaki, N., Mohamed, E.A. and Al Ashwal, H. (2018) Detecting social bots on Twitter: A literature review. Paper presented at 2018 International Conference on Innovations in Information Technology (IIT).

boyd, d. (2011) Social network sites as networked publics: Affordances, dynamics, and implications. In Z. Papacharissi (ed.), *A Networked Self: Identity, Community, and Culture on Social Network Sites.* New York: Routledge, pp. 39–58.

Bridgman, P. (1949) Einstein's theories and the operational point of view. In P.A. Schilpp (ed.), *Albert Einstein: Philosopher-Scientist.* La Salle, IL: Open Court, pp. 333–54.

Chen, Z., Tanash, R.S., Stollm, R. and Subramanian, D. (2017) *Hunting Malicious Bots on Twitter: An Unsupervised Approach.* In G.L. Ciampaglia, A. Mashhadi, and T. Yasseri (eds), *Proceedings of the International Conference on Social Informatics*, Cham: Springer, pp. 501–10.

Hall, S. (1980) Coding and encoding in the television discourse. In S. Hall, D. Hobson, A. Lowe and P. Willis (eds), *Culture, Media, Language: Working Papers in Cultural Studies.* London: Hutchinson, pp. 197–208.

Hartley, J. and Potts, J. (2014) *Cultural Science: The Evolution of Meaningfulness*. London: Bloomsbury.
Lewis, J. (2008) *Cultural Studies - The Basics*. London: Sage.
Lewis, J. and Best, K. (2003) The electronic polis: Media democracy and the invasion of Iraq. *Reconstruction: Studies in Contemporary Culture*, 3(3), pp. 297–319.
Pond, P. (2020a) *Complexity, Digital Media and Post Truth Politics: A Theory of Interactive Systems*. Cham: Palgrave Macmillan.
Pond, P. (2020b) An event-based model for studying network time empirically in digital media systems. *New Media & Society*, https://doi.org/10.1177/1461444820911711.
Pond, P. and Lewis, J. (2019) Riots and Twitter: Connective politics, social media and framing discourses in the digital public sphere. *Information, Communication & Society*, 22(2), pp. 213–31.
Thelwall, M. (2014) Sentiment analysis and time series with Twitter. In K. Weller, A. Bruns, J. Burgess, M. Mahrt and C. Puschmann (eds), *Twitter and Society*. New York: Peter Lang, pp. 83–95.
Weltevrede, E., Helmond, A. and Gerlitz, C. (2014) The politics of real-time: A device perspective on social media platforms and search engines. *Theory, Culture & Society*, 31(6), pp. 125–50.
Wojcik, S., Messing, S., Smith, A., Raine, L. and Hitlin, P. (2018) *Bots in the Twittersphere*. Washington, DC: Pew Research Center.

Index

www.ingramcontent.com/pod-product-compliance
Ingram Content Group UK Ltd.
Pitfield, Milton Keynes, MK11 3LW, UK
UKHW021056080625
459435UK00003B/17

* 9 7 8 1 0 3 2 0 0 4 4 8 8 *